MW00964770

Practical Ways to Good Health Through Traditional Chinese Medicine

China Today Press

Beijing 1997

Second Edition 1997

**Practical Ways to Good Health
Through Traditional Chinese Medicine**

China Today Press
(24 Baiwanzhuang Road, Beijing)
Postcode: 100037
Distributed by China International Book Trading Corporation
(35 Chegongzhuang Xilu, Beijing, China)
P. O. Box 399 Beijing, China Postcode: 100044

ISBN 7 − 5072 − 0902 − 4/R·20
14 − E − 2326P
02400

Editor's Note

Traditional Chinese medicine (TCM) is a treasure house in the country's fine cultural traditions. In its several thousand years of development it has accumulated rich experience in preventing and treating diseases. An especially important part of it is its scientific ways of keeping in good health.

This book on the practical ways to maintain good health is not an academic work. It describes for ordinary people the various simple ways of keeping fit and curing illnesses. How to sleep, diet, wear clothes, take a bath, maintain a healthy mood, have a normal sex life, as well as how to cure some common diseases such as insomnia and lumbago by yourself. Expensive drugs are not always necessary with diseases such as high blood pressure and cancer. Better is the prevention that can be had in everyday life — being optimistic and open-minded, scientific in diet, getting proper exercise, avoiding liquor and smoking.

Most of the articles in this book are contributed by teachers with the Beijing Institute of Traditional Chinese Medicine. Some have appeared in *China Today* (formerly *China Reconstructs*) and received favorable reactions. To meet the requests of readers we have compiled these into this book, adding more to make the content richer. Pictures and plates have been used to illustrate.

Practical is the word of this book. Every item is clearly explained, making it easy to follow. Keep trying for your health's sake and you will see good results.

Contents

Keeping Healthy with Good Living Habits

LIU ZHANWEN

T RADITIONAL Chinese medicine holds that good living habits, which aid the human organism in adjusting to the changes in natural environments, are important in preventing disease and maintaining good health.

Morning Principles

Ge Hong (284-364), a doctor of traditional Chinese medicine, wrote in his classic medical book that "people should not get up before the cock crows nor after sunset." This means that people should get up early and not oversleep. Traditional Chinese medicine believes that vital energy starts to accumulate in the morning and so advises people to do massage or other exercises in the morning to adjust the human organism.

The easiest way to do this is when you are still lying down. Before you get up, pat your chest several times. Then sit up, expel your breath sharply to let out the bad gas. Then rub your hands. When they become warm, "wash" your face with them. Use the back of your thumbs to rub the sides of your nose up and down 35 times. Then softly rub your upper eyelids 35 times. Embrace your head with your hands, palms covering your ears. Use your index and middle fingers to flip your head back 24 times. Swing your body right and left 35 times. Stretch each arm 35 times. Then stretch each leg 35 times. Finally, close each eye 35 times.

After getting up it is good to go to a park or riverside

Hu Yuanqing, 120, of Suizhou City, Hubei Province, is elected as a "Healthy Centenarian." He still does physical labor, goes to bed early and gets up early, and eats mainly vegetarian food.

where the air is fresh to do some mild exercises such as *qigong*, *taijiquan*, strolling or running. The negative ions of the fresh air help invigorate the metabolism and expel the harmful substances accumulated in your breathing during the night. Mild exercises also help achieve this effect. Old people should put on enough clothes to avoid being hit by cold or wind.

Proper Balance Between Work and Rest

In our daily life we must maintain a proper balance between work and rest. The Chinese people's ancestors suggested that we should harmonize the proportion between work and rest. Work leads to a healthy body. Sun Simiao, a noted Chinese doctor of ancient times, pointed out that proper manual and mental labor is important in building up the body and preventing disease. He advised old people to continually use their brain and to do physical exercises. But they should not be done to excess, otherwise they will ruin health.

However, to be too much at leisure can also damage health. More than 2,000 years ago, the Chinese classical medical book, *Yellow Emperor's Manual of Internal Medicine*, pointed out that excessive idleness harms health. This is because just idling away every day does not exercise the body and brain, hinders blood and vital energy circulation and produces flaccid muscles and indigestion. To balance work and rest one should first fix a regular time schedule for study, work and exercises. Then rest should consist of sleep and recreational activities. Try to develop different hobbies to enrich your life, such as listening to music, watching films or TV shows, enjoying poetry, painting, playing chess, and growing plants.

Bath Principles

Taking baths is one of the signs of civilization. They clean the skin, stimulate the blood circulation, expel fatigue and prevent disease. Many people who live long have the habit of taking frequent baths. Lukewarm or cold water is best. It's better

Li Ding, a lecturer with Shanxi Medical Academy, has compiled the first "Chart of Channels and Collaterals for Body-Shaping."

to have cold water in the morning or at noon than at night. Don't take a bath when you are hungry; it sometimes produces faintness from a decrease in blood sugar. On the other hand, if you take a bath when you are too full, your digestion will be affected.

Bathing time should not be too long nor the water too hot. Do not go into a breeze after a bath, for it is easy to catch a cold at this time. Those with coronary heart disease, angina pectoris or high blood pressure should be even more careful with a bath. Do not take a bath if you have a high temperature or have just been doing intense sports exercises. Menstruating or pregnant women should not take cold baths.

Sleep Principles

Sleep eliminates fatigue and restores energy. A Chinese saying claims that "to sleep well is better than to eat well." Nourishing food and tonics cannot replace the role of sleep. Traditional Chinese medicine advises people to go to bed early and get up early. Good sleep at night should be a habit. Don't often break this habit and work late into the night. The bed should not be too hard or too soft, and the pillow should not be too high. The best sleeping position is lying on your right side, supplemented by lying on your left side or back. Don't lie on your stomach. The bedroom should be clean and cosy.

If you are in a bad mood or unhappy, go out for a walk or do *qigong* or massage before going to bed. If conditions don't allow you to take a hot bath, washing your feet in warm water can also help sleep. Don't eat food, drink strong tea or coffee, or smoke before going to bed. While lying in bed, don't talk, lie in a breeze, or face the light. Don't open your mouth, cover your face with the blanket, lie in a damp place or in the open. In short, good sleeping habit is important to your health.

Laughter and Joy — the Best Medicine

LIU ZHANWEN

WHEN people become ill, the first idea that rolls through their mind is to see a doctor. They are seldom aware that their trouble may be caused by emotions. Modern medical research shows that many diseases afflicting adults are the result of emotional problems.

According to traditional Chinese medicine, emotional traumas are a major cause of disease. Over 2,000 years ago, the *Huangdi Neijing* (*Yellow Emperor's Manual of Internal Medicine*), China's first substantial medical work, said: "Five kinds of vital energies come from the five internal organs — joy, anger, sorrow, melancholy and fear. Joy hurts the heart, anger hurts the liver, brooding hurts the spleen, melancholy hurts the lungs and fear hurts the kidneys." What this meant is that emotional factors are natural human states, but that an excess of any of them can cause diseases. These diseases range from minor ones involving the hair to serious disorders affecting the entire body.

Chinese researchers on disease prevention attach great importance to the functions of the emotions in keeping physically fit and healthy. They theorize an interaction between the emotions and the body, believing that a good emotional state can help improve general well-being and increase longevity. Emphasis is placed on a peaceful state of mind and broadmindedness.

AS a popular Chinese proverb says, "A laugh makes you ten years younger and worry turns your hair gray."

Modern medical research has confirmed that of all the factors affecting health, one of the most harmful is extreme e-motion. People obsessed with melancholy, fear, sorrow, jealousy, shock and excitement for a long period of time, as well as those who ungergo prolonged periods of stress, are more likely to suffer high blood pressure, heart disease, mental disorders, asthma, chronic gastritis, glaucoma and, some researchers believe, even cancer. Women under these conditions are also more likely to have menstruation problems. Medical research from China and abroad shows that 70 percent of all gastritis cases and 80 to 90 percent of all headaches are related to the emotions. Recent medical experiments suggest that a bad state of mind, involving any of the emotions, plus stress may predispose a person to cancer — perhaps through a weakening of the defenses of the immune system.

A happy, peaceful mind is the most helpful factor for maintaining good health. When people are happy, their central nervous system works to strengthen their bodily functions, resulting in proper digestion and a strong metabolism. They have a good appetite and sleep well, thereby enjoying high spirits and a quick mind. Research also suggests that optimists may live longer than others. According to one survey of 372 centenarians, 98 percent had a cheerful and optimistic temperament. Doctors report that the wounds of a victor tend to heal more quickly than those of the defeated, and patients free from emotional burdens tend to recover from an illness sooner. If the patient is confident and optimistic about fighting the disease, he may recover sooner, and perhaps require less treatment. For patients in low spirits, an illness often lingers on or even worsens. So emotional factors may well have a direct effect on patients' recovery.

THE obvious question then is, how does one keep a positive state of mind? Here are some suggestions for achieving that goal:

1. Develop a strong sense of morality, an ethical code —

Energetic old women.

and live by it. People who are unselfish and noble-spirited are broadminded, optimistic and always in high spirits. Jealousy, envy, hate and anxiety are negative states that rebound on those who indulge in them.

2. Try to see the "broad picture" in life. Don't worry about small matters and don't be overly critical.

3. Love work and activity. Be devoted to it. One can find happiness in contributing to society. It is well known that some people fall into a depression after retirement, while those who keep active and have a cause or activity tend to be better off e-motionally and physically.

4. Exercise can invigorate the mind as well as the body. When you feel gloomy or angry, the best way to pull yourself out of those moods is through exercise.

5. Develop friendships and an openness to other people. Discussing your problems with friends can often lighten your spirits and give you a better perspective on things.

6. Cultivate a wide range of interests. Chess, calligraphy and painting are but a few of the many hobbies that can keep one's mind and body healthy. Music and other arts can take one out of one's self and give real emotional rewards.

F OR good health and longevity, you should learn to control your emotions, develop a carefree, relaxed lifestyle, and try to live in an atmosphere of good humor. Be cheerful and forget your worries — and live longer.

Live Longer by Obeying Nature

ZHANG HUDE

E VERYBODY wants to live a long time. Scientists now believe that human beings should be able to live to at least 120 years.

Traditional Chinese medicine over the centuries has developed special ways to follow the laws of nature in the four seasons to maintain good health and build up the body for a longer life. The early classic of traditional Chinese medicine, *Yellow Emperor's Manual of Internal Medicine*, said that "a wise way to preserve one's health is to conform to the changes in the four seasons and accordingly adjust one's living habits."

Many meteorological factors affect, in different degrees, body metabolism and internal secretion abilities through the function of the hypothalamus. These are temperature, humidity, atmospheric pressure, wind direction and speed, volume of rainfall, sunspots, cosmic rays and the movements of celestial bodies. Good weather checks the spread of disease and aids good health. Harsh weather often causes ailments. Based on this, traditional Chinese medicine has developed unique ways to adjust the body's internal organs in the four seasons, important doctrines in preserving good health.

Spring Therapy

In the spring people should go to sleep a bit later and get up a bit earlier. Outdoor exercises in the morning are necessary. Fresh air, the spring breeze and warm sun give people an ease of mind and high spirits.

People in China say, "Don't hasten to shake off your heavy clothes in the spring, but in the autumn put on more." Spring weather is changeable. As it gets warmer, the skin tends to become loose to suit the situation and its ability to resist cold drops. Thus, at this time weak and elderly people easily catch cold, which in turn often induces hidden illnesses. A Beijing College of Traditional Chinese Medicine investigation of 4,806 patients shows that March and April are the peak time for acute myocardial infarctions. So weak and elderly people should promptly put on more clothing when they feel cold and pay special attention to protecting the back.

All things come to life in the spring. Germs and viruses also begin to flourish, giving rise to pestilences. There are three ways to prevent acute diseases of spring. One, regularly drink broth prepared with the rhizome of crytomium, an herb that lessens inflammation and relieves internal heat or fever. Two, place peppermint oil in the bedroom. As this volatilizes it purifies the air. Three, persist in massage therapy exercises. Weak and elderly people should avoid going to public places where the air is contaminated.

Traditional Chinese medicine holds that the liver should not be so active in the spring. If it is too vigorous, it weakens and replaces the role of the spleen. Thus, in the spring sweet things that build up the spleen are encouraged, while sour food that strengthens the liver should be limited. Dates, rich in protein, sugar and vitamins B and C, are good for the spleen. The Chinese say, "Eat three dates a day and you won't grow old."

Summer Therapy

Nature becomes exuberant in the summer. People should adapt themselves to the weather, accumulating vital energy and raising resistance to disease for the coming winter. According to traditional Chinese medicine, in the summer people should go to bed late and get up early. They should maintain a happy mood and not lose their temper. It is ideal to live for a while at

Early morning fishing is beneficial to health.

A rest in a garden.

a seaside resort or a forest home.

In the summer one should avoid heat and exposure to the intense sun, staying in the lower temperature indoors. He must not sit or lie too long on damp cold ground just for momentary relief from the heat. Sweet-sour plum juice is a recommended drink. Families should prepare the "ten drops," *rendan* and other popular medicines for summer ailments. Rooms should be well ventilated. But do not sleep in a draught or with an electric fan on, let alone in the open. Keep air conditioners at medium level. Weak and elderly people must not stay too long in the shade of trees, pavilion above water or draughts, for these sometimes cause feet and hand numbness and Bell's palsy.

Traditional Chinese medicine advises people to restore and build up their internal energy in the spring and summer. To protect internal energy, one should refrain from eating too much cold fruit and vegetables and consuming too much cold drink. A hot dish is necessary at each meal. Also to protect internal energy, one should eat less greasy food but more light and easily digestible food. Porridges such as lotus leaf and mung bean porridge are good for elderly people.

Eight Ways to Resist Cancer

LIU ZHANWEN

C ANCER, heart and cerebral diseases are man's worst ene-
mies today. There are 20 million cancer victims in the
world, 5 million of whom die every year. In China 800,000
die of it annually, the second largest cause of death in the
country. Though the cause of cancer remains unclear, this does
not mean that we are helpless against it. Traditional Chinese
medicine holds that deficiency and stagnation of the circulation
of vital energy in the body are the main causes. To maintain an
exuberant vitality and keep fit can prevent cancer from devel-
oping. Here are eight ways in our daily life effective in resist-
ing cancer.

Be Optimistic

Scientific tests prove that mental irritation is vital to the
development of cancer because a bad mood weakens the body's
immunity and impairs the functions of the T-lymphocyte to resist the disease. To be healthy one has to be optimistic. Try to
control yourself and not flare up, not to be bothered by trifles
or fame and gain, to be large-minded and aboveboard. Develop hobbies to adjust and enrich your life.

Persist in Doing Exercises

Doctors of traditional Chinese medicine believe that invig-
orating the circulation of the blood is the clue to preventing
cancer, for this enhances the body's immunity. Exercises are

13

Morning exercises in the quiet of Beihai Park.

the best way to achieve this effect, for they stimulate blood flow and metabolism. Exercises permitted by the doctors after a cancer operation help check its spread to other parts of the body. Some cancer patients have found the symptoms disappearing as they continued doing exercises. For middle-aged and old people, the best exercises are *qigong, taijiquan*, running, walking, swimming and mountain climbing. The best times are morning or evening. Persist and the result will be distinct.

Pay Attention to Hygiene

As high as 80 to 90 percent of cancer is caused by environmental factors. Lung cancer, for example, is highly related to air pollution, and cancer of the liver to polluted water. Thus keeping good environmental sanitation is the best way to prevent the disease. Personal hygiene is important too. Waste gases, air and residue should be properly treated to avoid pollution. Care should be taken not to come in contact with radioactive rays. Infections should be treated promptly.

Rational Diet

Scientists believe that 50 percent of cancer incidence is caused by a diet containing carcinogenic substances. Thus a proper diet is also important in preventing cancer. Food should be varied, contain different vitamins, mineral substances and cellulose. Eat more fruit and vegetables, but less animal fat and salt.

Chew Carefully and Swallow Slowly

Chewing carefully when eating is necessary to fitness. This stimulates the secretion of saliva, a big aid in building up the body. Traditional Chinese medicine calls saliva "tonic jelly." Modern medicine has also proved that saliva influences metabolism in different parts of the body and aids development and immunity. Chew each mouthful 30 seconds and then any carcinogenic substance will lose its power. The good habit of chewing carefully will benefit you all your life. Old people without good teeth should be even more careful in chewing their food.

Health Food

Pay attention to the quality of your food. Some foods help raise the body's immunity and may aid in curing cancer. They include yoghurt, milk, bean products, royal jelly and mush-

15

rooms. Cabbage, tomatoes, cucumbers, spinach, turnips, carrots and bean sprouts are rich sources of vitamins A and C that help the body resist cancer and stimulate the secretion of interferon. Some contain ferments to resolve nitrosamine. Garlic, papaya, sweet potatoes and various kinds of tea also help prevent cancer.

No Smoking and Less Liquor

Smoking harms the body. The World Health Organization has repeatedly warned people not to smoke. Wine stimulates the circulation of the blood and causes the muscles and joints to relax. A little low-alcohol wine after a meal is good for health. But excessive drinking ruins health. Don't drink on an empty stomach. Old people and those with chronic diseases should drink still less.

Early Diagnosis

Cancer is not incurable. Early diagnosis and treatment is vital. In daily life one should pay attention to any abnormal signals and get early diagnosis and treatment. Prompt treatment should also be had with chronic diseases.

Prevention and health protection are important in tackling cancer. Persist in the above eight measures and you will gain good health.

Garlic as an Aid in Fighting Cancer

LIU JINZHOU

G ARLIC is an effective help in the prevention and treatment of cancer. Laboratory research in the United States indicates that the enzyme garlicin checks the growth of cancer cells. In clinical practice, Chinese doctors have gained similar results. At present, the preventive role of garlic is stressed.

It is known that germanium and selenium tend to prevent cancer. Garlic has a high content of these two trace elements. A healthy person's gastric juice has a high acidity. But those over 40 or with chronic gastric atrophy secrete less gastric acidity. Its PH value can drop to only 5, under such a condition inducing bacteria or moulds to develop in the stomach. Acted upon by these, the nitrate people take with food is reduced to nitrite, a major carcinogenic substance that composes nitrosamine. Garlic, however, controls the growth of bacteria and mould and thus can check the forming of nitrite, the necessary element for synthesizing nitrosamines.

Bacteria and mould are catalytic agents in the synthesis of dimethyl nitrosamine, diethyl sitrosamine and dibutyl nitrosamine. Without these agents synthesizing is difficult. Garlic stops bacteria and mould from acting as catalytic agents.

When the PH value of gastric juice is normal, nitrite and secondary amine undergo chemical reaction to form nitrosamine. Garlic acts on nitrite, preventing it from combining with secondary amine to form nitrosamine.

Carcinogenic substances exist in most people. But some

people develop cancer and some do not. This depends on the ability of a person to resist the disease. People in many countries eat garlic for their health. Its enzyme helps the digestion of fats and protein so they are easily assimilated. This is perhaps the reason garlic gives people a good appetite. Garlic contains glycoside that can control cholesterol and balance transaminase, two elements that also help prevent cancer. Doctors in Japan have discovered that cells treated with garlic preparations gain an enhanced immunity that stimulates the body to have an immunity reaction to wipe out cancer cells.

Thus facts show that eating garlic is a safe and effective way to help prevent cancer. An example is Cangshan County in China's Shandong Province, a main garlic growing area. Because its inhabitants eat much garlic, the mortality rate of cancer of the stomach there is the lowest in the province. Koreans love garlic and the incidence of cancer in that country is among the lowest in the world.

Careful chewing of the garlic brings out the full action of the enzyme garlicin which wipes out the bacteria and mould in the body that are the catalysts in the synthesization of the nitrosamines. When garlic is cooked, its enzyme is lost. The heat also damages other elements in garlic that prevent such synthesization. Pounded garlic should be eaten at once before its efficiency is lowered. Those who are not used to eating raw garlic can try sweet and sour garlic (garlic soaked in vinegar with sugar), though its efficiency is not the best.

Adults should eat 10 grams of garlic (4 cloves) a day. Results can be seen with time.

Food Therapy to Treat High Blood Pressure

ZHANG HUDE & BAO XINCHAO

T RADITIONAL Chinese medicine stresses that building up one's health is the fundamental necessity. Food therapy is an important way to do this. Diet therapy, noted a Qing Dynasty doctor of Chinese medicine, is ready at hand, leaves no side effects and the food itself is enjoyable.

Traditional Chinese medicine holds that high blood pressure is closely linked with the liver, as stated in *Yellow Emperor's Manual of Internal Medicine*. The disease is also thought to be affected by irrational eating and the lack of inner energy. Statistics show that the incidence of the disease among people who like fatty food is 8.1 percent, while for those who like light food it is only 2.4 percent. Mental workers have a higher incidence than manual workers.

Points for Attention

Three points must be observed in maintaining a proper diet for preventing high blood pressure.

1. Less liquor but more tea. Excessive alcohol in the body lowers the systolic function of the heart that, in turn, enhances the systole of the blood vessels of the internal organs. This causes a rise of blood pressure. The tannin in tea has the effect of vitamin E and strengthens the capillary walls. High blood pressure, therefore, is to that extent controlled. Constant drinking of tea reduces weight and blood lipoids. However, strong tea excites people and makes the heart beat faster.

2. Eat light food with less salt. The *Yellow Emperor's Manual of Internal Medicine* states that too much salt in the diet stagnates the blood circulation and even changes the blood color. Low fat, low cholesterol and low caloric food is recommended for patients with high blood pressure. They should especially take less salt. The incidence of high blood pressure with high salt intake is much higher than with low salt intake. Animal fat leads to plaque deposits in blood vessel walls, thus raising blood pressure.

3. Eat vegetable, vegetable oils and protein foods. The white of eggs, fish, lean pork, and bean products are high in protein necessary for good health. But don't overdo it and get fat. Vegetable oil promotes the oxidization of cholesterol into cholic acid, which is expelled from the body. Cholesterol thus can be lowered and the resiliency of the capillaries enhanced.

Nine Types of Food to Prevent High Blood Pressure

There is a great variety of food that helps prevent high blood pressure. The following are recommended.

1. Staple foods

Corn porridge. Eating corn porridge prevents constipation and helps expel cholic acid and thus lower the cholesterol level in the blood. Steam 100 grams of crushed corn or cook them into a gruel.

Lotus leaf porridge. Cook 50 grams of polished rice into a porridge. When it is almost ready, spread a lotus leaf on top and continue it over a slow fire for a few more moments. This porridge is specially recommended in hot summer, as it promotes the secretion of saliva and body fluid. It is good for the weak, old and fat who have high blood pressure and also patients who suffer from apoplexy.

Celery porridge. Wash a proper amount of celery and cut it into sections. Cook 50 grams of polished rice in a gruel. When it is almost done, put celery sections into it and continue to cook until the celery is soft. The porridge is ideal for breakfast. Laboratory tests show that celery can help lower high blood pressure and has a tranquilizing function. It is thus effective for overexcitement and headache in patients with high blood pressure.

2. Fruit

Watermelon. Both its juice and rind have a diuretic function and lower high blood pressure. Slowly boil down 12 grams of watermelon rind with 10 grams of Cassia tora and drink the broth as tea. It is effective in helping to lower high blood pressure. But those with a weak stomach and loose bowels should take less.

Bananas. Bananas tend to lower chronic disfunctioning of the internal organs. High blood pressure patients can eat up to five a day. It can be chopped and placed into a tea with sugar, a small cup three times a day.

Haw. This is effective in helping to lower high blood pressure. Slowly boil down 12 grams of haw or 7 grams of haw flowers into a gruel and drink it.

Persimmon. This fruit is good for lowering blood pressure. Cook ripe persimmon into a heavy mixture and take it with milk or rice water three times a day.

3. Aquatic products

Lotus seed pistil. Remove the plumule of the lotus and dry. Make 7 grams of broth with it and drink every day.

Kelp. Containing ammonia acid, it lowers blood pressure. Boil down 20 grams of kelp with 15 grams of Cassia tora and drink the soup or eat the kelp.

Jellyfish. Wash 200 grams of jellyfish and 600 grams of water chestnuts with skins. Boil down in a liter of water. When the water is down to about 250 grams, the broth is ready. It can be taken before or after meals. When blood pressure lowers to normal and symptoms have disappeared, reduce the frequency of taking it.

Mussels. Cook 10 grams of mussels and 30 grams of shepherd's purse or celery, and drink frequently.

4. Honey

Dissolve honey in lukewarm water and drink a half cup twice a day. Persistence gives better results.

5. Instant drinks

Wash 1,000 grams of corn tassel. Boil in water an hour and throw dregs away. Continue to boil over low fire until the broth becomes concentrated. Remove from fire and let cool. Add 500 grams of powdered sugar to take up the remaining water. Stir until smooth, then dry it. Crush into small pieces and put into bottles for use. Three times a day dissolve 10 grams in water and drink. Corn tassel is a diuretic and helps to lower blood pressure.

Blue dogbane. Wash 500 grams of the leaves. Boil 20 minutes in water, strain off juice, add more water and boil again. Repeat this three times. Throw away the dregs. Combine the juice of the different times and slowly boil it over a low fire until concentrated. Let cool. Add 500 grams of powdered sugar to take up remaining water. Stir smooth, let dry and crush, placing crystals in bottle. Each time dissolve 10 grams in boiling water and drink as tea.

Chrysanthemum and Cassia tora. Put 3 grams of clean, dry chrysanthemum flower, 15 grams of raw haw slices, and 15 grams of Cassia tora into a thermos bottle. Pour boiling water in and cover to steep for half an hour. Drink several times a day.

6. Meal dishes

Stewed beef with tomatoes. Clean 250 grams of tomatoes and cut into even pieces. Slice 100 grams of beef. Stew both with vegetable oil, salt and sugar. Serve.

Steamed eggplant. Put two clean eggplants, a little vegetable oil and salt on a plate and steam it. Serve.

Spinach with sesame oil. Clean 250 grams of spinach. Boil three minutes in water with a little salt. Pour sesame oil over it, mix and serve.

7. Soup

Crystal sugar and vinegar soup. Put 100 milliliters of vinegar and 500 grams of crystal sugar in a bottle. Shake until the sugar is dissolved. Take a spoonful after each meal. This is good for high blood pressure patients whose body fluid is insufficient or have blood stagnancy. Do not take this if you have stomach trouble.

8. Tea

Chrysanthemum tea. Put 10 grams of dried chrysanthemum petals and 3 grams of Dragon Well tea (or other green tea) in a cup. Add boiling water and cover to steep. It is ready in a minute or so.

Black fungus tea. This is sour but fragrant. Add sugar and more water to taste. Take 150 milliliters three times a day. If you have stomach trouble, drink it only after meals.

9. Others

Garlic. In the morning before breakfast eat one or two garlic segments soaked in vinegar. The vinegar in which they have been soaked can also be taken. Two weeks of this should show results in lowering blood pressure.

Peanuts. The skin of peanuts helps lower blood pressure and cholesterol level. Boil the peanut skins and take 150 grams of the broth as tea morning and night. The tender leaves of the peanut plant can be substituted for peanut skins. You can also soak raw peanuts in vinegar and eat 20 of them morning and evening. The peanuts themselves also help lower blood pressure.

Diet for Diabetes

ZHANG HUDE

DIABETES is caused by the deficiency of insulin secretion which leads to the disturbance of the sugar metabolism in the body. When the body cannot assimilate sugar normally, it is retained in the blood, showing an increase in blood sugar. When the amount of blood sugar exceeds the kidney threshold, glucose will be discharged in the urine.

When sugar is discharged from the kidneys, it brings with it much liquid, increasing the amount of urine and at the same time raising the patient's demand for water. Since much glucose is lost and sugar in the body cannot be fully consumed, the patient easily feels hungry. He tires easily and becomes emaciated.

Diabetes can be contracted by children and old people, those over 40 more frequently than children under ten. Generally more office workers than laborers and more city residents than rural people are likely to have it. If parents are diabetics, their children in many cases also contract it, for the disease is hereditary.

Traditional Chinese medicine acknowledged the disease as early as 200 B.C. when the *Yellow Emperor's Manual of Internal Medicine* was written, in which the symptoms of diabetes were recorded. Traditional Chinese medicine considers the cause of diabetes as too much fat and sugar, which results in an increase of inner heat. It is also caused by anger, sadness and other irritants which are turned into internal fire that burns up *yin* liquid in the lungs, stomach and spleen.

The first step to treating any diabetic is the control of the diet. The key is to limit the intake of carbohydrates, grain and sugar. Minor cases can generally recover through diet control. Even serious cases can be stabilized this way. Unrestricted eating will worsen the condition. Diet control is a must.

I. Diet

Diabetics must strictly control their sugar intake. They should eat none or little of such foods as desserts, fruit juice and potatoes (starch). When they do eat these, they must cut down on their main food grain as an exchange. The usual amount of main food per day is 200 to 250 grams for those who do not work, 250 to 300 grams for light manual laborers, 300 to 400 grams for average laborer, and 400 grams or more for heavy laborers. Extremely bitter, cold or hot food should be avoided.

Because of metabolic disturbance, the decomposition of protein is faster and much is lost. Therefore diabetics should eat more protein-rich foods such as milk, eggs, fish, lean meat and bean products. Generally one kilogram of weight needs 1 to 1.5 grams of protein. For average patients the total intake of fat is 50 to 60 grams a day. But overweight patients cannot take more than 40 grams per day. To help prevent arteriosclerosis, diabetics should use vegetable oil and limit food that contain high cholesterol. They should eat little roe, brains, yolk, fat and animal internal organs. Because they eat less grain, their intake of vitamin B1 becomes less and they should eat foods that contain this vitamin to make up for it. Otherwise they might get disease of the nervous system. Fresh fruit and vegetables are also good for them. A small amount of honey taken on a regular basis can help lower the blood sugar.

The process of recovery through diet control is slow. Practitioners should keep the patient steady with it.

II. Herbal Medicines

Traditional Chinese medicine prescriptions for diabetes are based on the degrees of the three main symptoms and the distinction of kidney weakness from lung fire and stomach heat.

For all patients, the diet should be light. Sweet, heavy, hot or other pungent food and alcohol are forbidden. Proper diet is usually accompanied by herbal medicine in all cases of diabetes.

1. Prescription for Cases with Upper-Body Symptoms

Symptoms: The mouth is dry and the tongue feels hot. The tongue is yellow coated and red at the edge and tip. The pulse is strong and fast, and the patient drinks and urinates much more than normal. Treatment should help bring fever down, moisten the lungs, promote the secretion of saliva and slake thirst.

Prescription 1: Chinese Trichosanthes (*Trichosanthes kirilowii*)

Roots and Chinese Yam Gruel

Wash 15 grams of Chinese trichosanthes roots, 10 grams of Chinese yam, and 30 grams of rice. Put in a pot and add three bowls of cold water. Boil for 20 minutes and then add a teaspoon of honey.

Dose: One bowlful twice a day for two months.

Prescription 2: Five-juice Drink

Mix proper amount of fresh reed rhizome, peeled pear, peeled water chestnuts, fresh lotus root and fresh tuber of dwarf lilyturf. Drain the juice and drink it cold or hot. No limit.

Prescription 3: Pear Juice

Slice a big juicy pear. Soak the slices in cold water for 12 hours. Drink the water frequently.

2. Prescriptions for Cases with Middle-Body Symptoms

Symptoms: The patient eats a lot, gets hungry and thirsty easily and becomes emaciated. Bowel movements are hard and dry, and urination is frequent. Pulse is thready but strong. Treatment should be aimed at moistening the stomach, smoothing bowel movements, building up the *yin*, and protecting body fluid.

Prescription 1: Clam and Balsam Pear Soup

Use 250 grams of balsam pear and 100 grams of live clams (the clams should have been soaked in fresh water two days) to make a soup. Flavors can be added as desired. Consume all.

Research reports show that balsam pear is of cool and cold nature and tastes bitter-sweet. It can lower the amount of blood sugar, relieve thirst and internal heat and fever, and reduce irritability. Clams taste sweet and salty and are of cold nature. It can relieve thirst and internal heat and fever, build up the *yin* and smooth the flow of urine. The two combined are especially good for cases with strong symptoms of stomach fever and *yin* weakness.

Prescription 2: Kudzu Vine Root, Chinese Dates and Mung Bean Soup

Soak ten Chinese dates in warm water for a half hour. Put the dates and 30 grams of clean kudzu vine roots in an earthenware pot. Add two and a half bowls of water. Boil down for a half hour. Keep dates and juice only in the pot. Add 50 grams of mung beans and simmer for 40 minutes.

Dose: One bowlful twice a day. The soup cannot be kept over night.

Prescription 3: The Root of Membranous Milk Vetch (*Astragalus membranaceus*) and Chinese Yam Soup

Boil down 30 grams of the roots and 30 grams of Chinese yam. Drink it as tea.

It is reported that the roots of membranous milk vetch control sugar in the body. Noted doctor of Chinese medicine Zhu Chenyu considers that because roots of membranous milk vetch invigorate the stomach, promote vital energy and *yang*, while Chinese yam can promote vital energy and *yin* and strengthen the kidneys, when they are combined they promote vital energy and the secretion of body fluid, build up the spleen and kidneys, lower sugar in the urine, relieve emissions, preserve the essence of the diet. and turn sugar in urine negative.

3. Prescriptions for Cases with Lower-Body Symptoms

Symptoms: The patient urinates a lot and the urine is thick

and turbid, and in some cases sweet. The mouth is dry, producing little saliva, and the tongue is red. The pulse is thin and fast. Treatment helps reinforce body fluid, nourish the blood, and strengthen the kidneys.

Prescription 1: Stew of Chinese Wolfberry and Rabbit

Use 15 grams of Chinese wolfberry and 250 grams of rabbit meat to make a stew. Eat the meat and drink the juice.

The fruit of the Chinese wolfberry can lower blood sugar and rabbit meat can relieve thirst and the need to urinate. The two combined can invigorate the liver and kidneys, build up the spleen and relieve thirst. It is especially good for diabetics with strong symptoms of weakness of liver and kidneys.

Prescription 2: Pigskin Soup

Boil 500 grams of pigskin until it is tender. Remove the skin and add 30 grams of honey and 250 grams of rice flour. Boil slowly until done. Drink it three times a day for two days.

This prescription is adopted from *Shanghan Lun* (*Treaties on Fevers*), originally used for deficiency of the *yin*, and diarrhea caused by it, sore throat and the bloating of the chest. It is used for diabetes because of its function in reinforcing body fluid and nourishing the blood.

Prescription 3: Sparrow and Medicine Gruel

Slowly boil down 30 grams of dodder seeds and 30 grams of Chinese wolfberry in an earthenware pot. Keep the liquid. Stir-fry five cleaned sparrows in cooking wine. Boil the cooked sparrows and 100 grams of rice in the juice. When it is about done, add salt, ginger and the white of a green Chinese onion. Drink the gruel.

Traditional Physical Therapy for Diabetes

YUAN LIREN

DIABETES exhibits three main symptoms: frequent eating, drinking and urination. Traditional Chinese medicine believes that it is caused by inner heat and the decrease of the circulation of vital energy and the blood caused by old age. Therefore, physical therapy in addition to medication is suggested.

The physical therapy has two steps.

FIRST, lie down on the bed and loosen the clothes. Stretch the back and at the same time draw a deep breath. Inhale to the maximum, hold the breath for two seconds and then exhale slowly. When breathing, the tip of the tongue should touch the palate lightly. Do this five times.

In this first step the person should be quiet, relaxed and concentrated so that the air can circulate smoothly in the lungs. It is recommended that it be done either in the morning or in the evening.

Though the method seems simple, it exercises internal organs and invigorates the blood circulation and the process of metabolism. A deep breath enables the vital energy to reach every part of the body. When it reaches the spleen, this organ is strengthened and will be able to accelerate the circulation of blood and vital energy, which in turn helps enhance the circulation of body fluid. When the vital energy circulation is smooth and the body fluid is plentiful, the mouth and throat will be moistened and *yin* weakness and inner heat will be re-

29

Tianjin: *Taijiquan* exercises in the morning.

duced, thus reducing the symptoms of diabetes. The movements seem inactive but all the movements take place inside the body.

S ECOND, the person should walk 120 steps and up to a thousand, depending on his general health. The purpose is to exercise the body and smooth the main and collateral channels. This invigorates the circulation of the blood, vital energy and body fluid, strengthens the joints and enhances metabolism. It coordinates with the first step, harmonizing internal organs with the body itself. It is especially good for elderly diabetics.

The method should not be used directly after a meal or with an empty stomach because at these times the blood and vital energy can easily be consumed, which is harmful to the body. If the person feels weak or exhausted during the exercise, he should stop until he feels normal again.

T HIS physical therapy has a good effect on the efficacy of other treatment being used for diabetes. In recent years some foreign doctors have begun to recognize this. In Malmo, Sweden, doctors planned physical exercises for their diabetic patients. Three months later their condition had greatly improved and at last all of them recovered. The American book *The Therapeutics of Diabetes* also suggests that physical exercises should be fitted into regular medical treatment.

This physical therapy has existed in China for over a thousand years and should be promoted. The results should be considerable.

Traditional Dietary Beauty Aids

WENG WEIJIAN

S INCE ancient times the quest for beauty and the secret of prolonging youth have commanded man's attention. A vast array of beauty aids have been developed throughout the world. An ancient Chinese work, *Shan Hai Jing* (*Canon of Seas and Mountains*), mentions bathing in medicinal herbs, while *Shennong Bencao Jing* (*Shennong Materia Medica*), an early medical text, lists dozens of foods and herbs used to improve appearance.

According to traditional Chinese medicine, the condition of the skin and the smell of the breath are reliable indicators of a person's general health. A poor complexion is believed to be caused by an imbalance in the body's fluids. It is essential for good health to restore this balance by improving the functioning of the internal organs. This in turn leads to a healthy, clear complexion.

The following are some of the more common types of poor complexion or skin tone. Each is followed by a simple remedy.

Pallor

Extreme pallor may indicate that the patient is suffering from anemia, general weakness after childbirth, blood loss, fatigue, shortness of breath, poor appetite, insomnia, edema (swelling) of the legs, diarrhea, or other more serious conditions. A tonic made of honey, Chinese dates, and peanuts may be beneficial. Take 100 grams of Chinese dates and 100 grams of peanuts and soak in warm water. Simmer until soft. Add 200 grams of honey and simmer further until liquid is reduced. Taken frequently this tonic will increase vitality and improve the complexion.

Dull complexion

Those with grayish, lackluster skin may be suffering from some form of wasting disease, a low-grade fever, aching back and legs, or sexual problems. Traditionally, these conditions are associated with malfunctioning of the kidneys. A tonic made from chestnuts and cabbage is beneficial for the kidneys, and can help increase vitality.

Take 200 grams of raw, shelled chestnuts, and slice in half. Boil in 500 ml of duck broth until soft. Add 200 grams of cabbage, salt and monosodium glutamate (MSG) to taste. When the cabbage is cooked, pour in a little cornstarch mixed with water. Remove from heat and stir until smooth.

Rough skin

People with rough and wizened skin are believed to generate excessive body heat or they may be in the later stages of a high fever. They may also suffer from a dry throat, thirst, restlessness, and constipation. All these can be caused by a reduced blood volume or excessive body heat.

Bamboo shoots help to reduce body temperature, while sea cucumber assists in blood formation. Take 200 grams of sea cucumber and 100 grams of bamboo shoots, slice, and soak in water. Boil in 500 ml of lean meat broth. Add salt, sugar, soy, yellow wine and a little cornstarch. Stir until the soup becomes smooth. This soup may help bring back smoothness and luster to dry skin.

Wrinkles

Disorders of the spleen or the kidneys are believed to cause premature wrinkling of the forehead, and around the eyes and neck. They can also cause the skin of the whole body to become slack, making the patient look much older than his or her years. The patient may also tire easily and suffer from backache and weakness in the legs.

Chinese yams have for generations had the reputation of prolonging life. They also help correct imbalances in the spleen and the kidneys. Walnut kernels are good for the kidneys and the brain, and Chinese dates fortify the blood. Haws and green plums benefit the spleen and the stomach by stimulating appetite and aiding digestion.

Take 500 grams of freshly skinned Chinese yams. Boil until soft and mash. Form into a round flat cake. Place walnut pieces, Chinese dates, haws and green plums on the surface of the cake and steam. Serve with hot honey.

Puffiness of the face

Defective kidneys often cause puffiness of the face and swelling in the legs. Sufferers may often appear pale, and experience shivering, backaches, and urinary frequency.

The leaves of the rapeseed plant (colza) act as a diuretic when made into a soup with shrimp and chicken. They promote health and help reduce swelling.

Swollen neck or double chin

Haws improve circulation of the blood and can help to eliminate fatty tissue. Honey contains plenty of fructose which is more easily metabolized than ordinary sugar, and so less likely to lead to the formation of fat deposits.

Take 500 grams of raw haws, wash, discard stems and kernels. Boil with water until the haws are soft and almost all the liquid has evaporated. Pour in 200 grams of honey and simmer until slightly reduced.

Swollen eyelids

Swollen eyelids is believed to be caused by lessened blood volume and vital energy, stagnation of humidity and poor circulation of the blood. These conditions are always associated with fatigue, insomnia and swelling of the legs.

A tonic made of an edible fungus, mushrooms and egg-plant may be beneficial. Use 200 grams of eggplant, 20 grams of soaked edible fungus and fresh mushrooms. Deep-fry diced eggplant first. Boil in chicken soup together with fungus and mushrooms. Add soy sauce, sugar, salt, and a bit of cornstarch. Stir until the soup becomes smooth.

Dark orbits

These are associated with palpitation, insomnia, backache and fatigue.

A tonic made of Chinese wolfberry and yellow croaker is held to be beneficial. Take a 1-kilogram yellow croaker, scale, gut and remove the bones, head and tail. Dip the fish in flour paste and fry until it becomes yellow. Put on a tray. Pour some oil into a frying pan and heat, add soy sauce, sugar, vinegar, yellow wine, 50 grams of wolfberry, diced cucumbers, pota-toes and a bit of cornstarch. Stir until it thickens. Pour this on the fish.

Sebaceous dermatitis

Most such patients are strong young and middle-aged peo-ple who have halitosis, hydrochor hydria, stomach upset and heated blood.

Balsam pears are believed to be good for reducing fever and thus good for this condition. Use 250 grams of pears, wash, remove seeds and cut into slivers. Fry in vegetable oil with a few carrot slivers. Add salt and a bit of cornstarch. Go with rice or bread.

Freckles

People with freckles are mostly women with fair complex-ions. The cause is considered to be disorders of the liver and kidneys, and the rise of weakness heat, and is associated with dry throat, thirst, backache and low fever.

A tonic made of soft-shelled turtle and artemisia

(*Artemisia apiacea*) is beneficial. Take a soft-shelled turtle (1 kilogram), remove head, legs and organs, and dice. Add 20 grams of prepared artemisia in small pieces ready for decoction, plus salt, water and yellow wine. Simmer gently.

Skin spots

Skin spots occur mostly in women, especially pregnant women with rib pain, diarrhea and weakness of the spleen. Sometimes these are associated with dysmenorrhea, amenorrhea and vomiting during pregnancy.

A tonic made of fingered citron and tender tips of bamboo shoots may be good for the liver and spleen. Use fresh tips of bamboo shoots, 20 grams of prepared fingered citron in small pieces ready for decoration, and 20 grams of ginger. Slice and boil in an earthenware pot until they are cooked. Remove from fire, add salt and steep for 24 hours. Take frequently.

Acne

This occurs mostly in young people who may also suffer from disorder of the kidneys, stomach heat and the accumulation of bodily humidity.

Considered beneficial for this are three dishes made with Chinese toon, beancurd and eggs. (The toon leaves may be fresh or salted.)

1. Fried leaves of Chinese toon. Cut the toon leaves up and mix with flour paste. Add salt and fry in vegetable oil.

2. Mixed leaves of toon and beancurd. Steam beancurd first. Mix it with toon leaves, add salt and sesame oil.

Steamed toon leaves and eggs. Cut up toon leaves, beat eggs and mix with leaves. Add salt and fry in vegetable oil.

Acne rosacea

This is always associated with halitosis and yellow urine. Patients are fond of cold drinks. The cause is mainly humidity and heat of the lungs and stomach.

A tonic made of the rinds of watermelon, wax gourd and

cucumber is beneficial for the lungs and stomach. Use 200 grams of watermelon rind, 300 grams of wax gourd rind and 400 grams of cucumber rind. Wash and boil separately. Let cool and slice. Put them in a container then add salt. Soak for 12 hours.

Aged marks

People with aged marks are suffering from blood loss, shortness of breath or sexual problems. These conditions are associated with body weakness, thinness, easy fatigue, dry and itching skin, and constipation.

A tonic made of quail eggs and tremella helps. It requires 50 grams of tremella that has been soaked in water, and 8 cooked quail eggs. Put in a pot, add chicken soup, salt, and yellow wine. Simmer until soft. This is especially good for old people.

Weight-Reducing with Diet

ZHANG SUXIN

O BESITY is caused mainly by taking in too many calories. Exercise and proper diet help take off those excess pounds without side effects of medicines. Weight can be reduced through physical labor and exercise, for these stimulate catabolism and the consumption of fat and the synthesis of muscle protein. But it is a proper diet that controls the amount of calories one takes in.

Here are important points to keep in mind when following a weight-reducing diet:

1. Keep the amount of calories taken each day at the lowest level. This can be determined with your doctor, who will calculate your daily calorie need according to your weight and amount of movement. If you are not too overweight, you can adjust the amount of calories yourself according to results of practice.

For those who are only a little fat it is enough to moderate only a little in eating and drinking. This can reduce weight by a half to a kilogram a month. If this does not work, try to reduce the amount of food you eat until it produces the effect, then persist with this level.

A diet that confines calories to 1,400 Kcal. is:

Breakfast: — A large bowl of jellied beancurd
— A cake (50 grams)
— One egg stewed in tea
Lunch: — Steamed buns stuffed with meat, cabbage and Chinese chive. (75 grams flour, 50 grams lean

meat, 100 grams cabbage and a pinch of chive)

— Corn gruel made of 25 grams of cornflour.

— Sliced radish with carrots flavored with salt

Supper: — Millet gruel (50 grams)

— Steamed bread (50 grams)

— Fried sliced beef and celery in vegetable oil (25 grams beef, 250 grams celery, 5 grams oil)

— One egg stewed in soy sauce

People whose weight surpasses normal by 10 percent must strictly confine their daily calorie intake within 1,200 Kcal. and try to reduce their weight by 0.5 to 1 kilogram each week. If there is no change after two weeks, reduce the daily limit to 1,000 Kcal.

A diet for a 1,200 Kcal. limit is:

Breakfast: — Soybean milk (250 ml.)

— A cake (25 grams)

— A deep-fried dough cake (25 grams)

— One boiled egg

Lunch: — Oatmeal porridge (25 grams of oatmeal)

— Cake baked with 50 grams of flour

— Spiced fish (50 grams)

— Quick fried celery and carrot in hot oil, then boiled with soy sauce and water (300 grams)

Supper: — Rice gruel (25 grams)

— Steamed twisted roll (50 grams)

— Mixed kelp and cucumber (100 and 200 grams) flavored with garlic, soy sauce, vinegar and salt.

— One boiled egg

A diet for keeping below 1,000 Kcal. is:

Breakfast: — A large bowl of jellied beancurd

— A sesame seed cake (50 grams)

— One boiled egg

Lunch: — Steamed twisted roll (20 grams cornflour, 20 grams wheat flour)

— Braised beef seasoned with soy sauce (50 grams)

— Fried bean sprouts and Chinese chive (250 grams sprouts, 50 grams chive)

— Tomato and wax gourd soup (50 grams tomato, 100 grams gourd)

Supper: — Steamed cake (50 grams)

— Fried sliced meat and rape (250 grams rape, 25 grams meat)

— Summer radish and coriander soup (100 grams radish, a little coriander)

Those whose weight is 20 percent above normal will feel unwell and suffer tiredness, palpitation and shortness of breath, or complications such as heart trouble, hypertension and diabetes. The calorie intake every day must be lower than 800 Kcal. in order to reduce the weight quickly. If this does not work, then under a doctor's supervision, try intermittent starvation therapy.

2. Limiting daily calory intake mainly means cutting the amount of carbohydrates and fat. Sugar and foods made with sugar, animal oil and wine and liquors are strictly forbidden. It is necessary to take in a certain amount of food made of coarse grains which provide sufficient vitamins and inorganic salts but contain low calories. It is better to take even less vegetable oil.

3. Reducing the daily amount of calories not only reduces body fat but consumes protein and other not-fats. Therefore enough protein should be eaten. The amount of protein needed is determined according to a person's weight — usually one gram of protein per kilogram of body weight. The ideal foods for protein intake include bean products, eggs, dairy products, fish, fowl and lean meat.

4. To ease the hunger that accompanies weight reducing diets, eat various low-calorie vegetables. If this does not work, eat foods that expand, such as popcorn.

5. If possible, have many meals a day but little food each time to avoid a hyperactive appetite.

Rice Is a Medicine

DU LINGFANG

R ICE is becoming a favorite with foreign nutritionists today. In European and American countries where bread is a traditional food, it is being used in medication for weight control and some diseases.

In the United States, rice is considered one of the best diet foods. There are books that talk about its benefit on health and the beauty of the body. An American doctor, after first using the therapy for diabetes in 1939, is using a rice diet therapy to treat obesity. Another American nutritionist says that brown rice is valuable anti-cancer food.

As a matter of fact, many classic Chinese medical books speak of rice being used as medicine. The *Compendium of Materia Medica* by Li Shizhen (1518-1593) says that rice is of a sweet and cool nature, and contains neutralized vital energies of heaven and earth, and that it invigorates the stomach.

Rice is also nourishing. It is good for the spleen, stomach and lungs. Traditionally, Chinese doctors prescribed medicines to be cooked in rice. This method is especially helpful for those who are recovering from illness when their stomach is weak. Water left over from washing uncooked rice can also be frozen and then used to heal ulcerated corners of the mouth, for when it is applied it creates a protective membrane that subdues inflammation.

Rice crust (formed in the bottom of the pot in which it is cooked) helps cure indigestion, diarrhea, and weakness and coldness of the spleen and stomach. The Chinese herbal medicine "rice crust pill" is used for infant indigestion. A research project conducted by the Singapore National University

The Heilongjiang Province Elders Festival.

showed that thin rice gruel is very effective for infant diarrhea and dehydration, more effective than oral electrolytic solution recommended by World Health Organization. The researchers therefore recommended that rice gruel replace such solutions as standard prescriptions for infant diarrhea.

Present studies of nutrition show that rice contains amino acids, unsaturated fatty acid, the vitamin B family, cellulose and various trace elements such as calcium, phosphorus, magnesium, selenium and iron, all necessary to the body. Rice has low calories and low fat, and contains compound carbohydrates that give the stomach a feeling of fullness, which can help in the cure of obesity.

People in the north should also eat rice in order to keep a balanced and diversified diet, and prevent deficient nutrition. Young parents in particular should remember that thin rice gruel has a special effect on health protection and disease prevention in children.

Spring Exercises for Keeping the Liver Fit

YUAN LIREN

A S SPRING returns, all earthly things come back to life. The change of nature affects the activities of human life. People take part in more activities and metabolism becomes exuberant. This means that both blood circulation and the supply of nutrition need to be quickened and increased. The acceleration of blood circulation depends mainly on the readjustment of the blood volume, but the increase in nutrients needs good digestion and absorption.

According to traditional Chinese medicine, these functions have something to do with the liver, which stores blood and produces it. The liver can also control people's feelings, playing an important role in digestion and absorption. In the spring, people can adapt to the changes in the natural world so long as they keep the physiological function of the liver vigorous. This is why Chinese doctors believe it is good to do liver-preservation exercises in the spring.

There are many ways to take care of the liver. First, people should be optimistic and happy, and expand as things develop. Depression and anger harm the liver. Those who get up early and go to bed early will be full of vigor. For proper vital energy and blood condition, clothes must be warm, loose and comfortable. As for diet, wheat, dates, oranges, peanuts, o-nions and coriander are good for spring. Eat less raw and cold food made of glutinous rice, which damages the stomach and spleen. In physical exercise, take part in more outdoor activities so as to absorb the vitality of nature. Exercises should be slow and smooth, such as *taijiquan*, *qigong* and "eight-section exercises." In the spring when the grass has just turned green, go on outings, go for a walk in the country, listen to the birds singing in the forest, and enjoy the scenery by the waterside. These help you get rid of worry, mould your temperament, limber the joints and give you more fresh air.

Simple Liver-Preservation Exercises

1. Stretching. Early in the morning as you wake up and stretch, you will feel extremely pleasant, and this will also do you good physically. After a night's sleep people usually feel slack and weak. Blood circulation is slower. Stretching your arms and legs, waist and abdomen while inhaling and exhaling helps get rid of the stale and take in the fresh. It invigorates the circulation of the blood and vital energy, and frees the main and collateral channels. Stretching relieves fatigue, shakes off drowsiness, builds up strength and limbers the body.

"The blood stays in the liver when a person lies in bed, but circulates when a person moves," traditional Chinese medicine says. Stretching speeds blood circulation, limbers the body and awakens you. It stimulates the function of the liver. This can also be repeated twice before or after a nap. Old people doing it can increase the elasticity of the muscles and ligaments and help postpone aging.

2. Pressing the palms while turning the waist. Sit straight with legs separated and one hand on the other between the legs. With the palms downward, the arms are kept straight and pressed downward with force while turning the waist left and right slowly four times.

Attention: The turning range should be short. It is enough if you feel a resistance as you turn your waist while pressing your palms downward. These exercises have the same effect as stretching yourself; they stimulate the circulation of vital energy and blood, and limber the joints.

3. Take a sitting position. With one hand holding the oth-

45

er, place your hands in front of your chest and pull them outward four times. Then turn your palms upward and downward
five times.

Attention: Inhale as you exert yourself and exhale as you
relax. This has the same effect as the above exercises.

Exercises for the Heart in the Summer

YUAN LIREN

I T IS in the summer that all living things flourish the most and the human body's metabolism is most active. In the long days, short nights and hot weather, people have more outdoor activity and less sleep. Higher energy consumption means quicker blood circulation, more sweat and a heavier burden on the heart. Neglect of proper maintenance of the heart is harmful. So traditional Chinese medicine stresses care of the heart in the summer.

There are many ways to protect the heart. For example, going to bed later in the evening and getting up earlier in the morning; wearing lighter clothing and changing more often; eating less warm food and more sour, sweet and spicy food to make up for excess sweating; and keeping in a good mood. Here are some exercises for keeping the heart healthy:

1. Sit straight. Place the two arms between the thighs naturally. Breathe evenly. Then make fists, exhale when clenching and inhale when loosening. Repeat six times without interruption.

This exercise can regulate the *qi* (vital energy) and blood flow. Exerting strength following the breath is beneficial to the normal functioning of the channels and collaterals through which the *qi* circulates. When making fists, the movements of the fingers can massage the *laogong* points at the center of the palms, which is good for heart maintenance. A better result can be had by grasping a keep-fit ring in each hand.

2. Sit straight. Use the left hand to press the right wrist.

Breathe evenly. Raise the two hands above the head as if lifting something heavy. Exhale when the hands are up and inhale when they are down. Repeat 10 to 15 times. Then put the right hand on the left wrist and do the same. Also repeat 10 to 15 times.

This exercise can promote the normal operation of channels and collaterals, regulate the *qi* and blood flow, and limber the muscles and joints of the arms.

3. Sit straight. Clasp the two hands. Bend the right knee, put the knee between the two palms. Exert strength against the knee, then relax. Change to the left knee and do the same. Repeat six times each.

This exercise can treat ailments in the chest area and make one feel relieved. It can also limber the muscles and joints of the limbs.

4. Sit straight. Place the two arms on the knees naturally. Close the eyes slightly. Breathe evenly. Close mouth slightly. Sit still for a while. When the saliva accumulates, swallow it in three gulps. Then clamp the teeth 10 to 15 times.

This exercise can tranquilize the nerves, strengthen the teeth and invigorate the function of the spleen.

Points to remember: Do the exercises in a quiet place with cool, fresh air. Early morning or in the evening is best. Elderly people, weak and those with heart troubles should do more in the summer.

Exercises for Lung Health in the Autumn

YUAN LIREN

T HE weather turns cooler when autumn begins. In the changeable climate people are liable to catch colds and there are more occurrences of cough and asthma. Those who have had asthma for long often have attacks in this season. Traditional Chinese medicine observes the weather's influence on human health and believes that in autumn the *qi* (vital energy) of the lungs is liable to be injured. It recommends paying attention to the changes of the weather, protecting the *qi* of the lungs, and thus avoiding colds and coughing.

There are many ways to protect the lungs. For example, going to bed earlier and getting up earlier, the former to avoid colds and the latter to enjoy fresh air; wearing suitable clothing according to the changes of weather; and eating more warm food with enough fluid and less spicy food. Here are some exercises to help keep the lungs healthy.

1. Sit straight in a relaxed way. Breathe evenly. Cross the legs naturally, bend the waist, use the hands to support the body and raise the body 5 times without stopping. Repeat the exercise 3 times.

Points to remember: Exert enough force on th arms. Hold the breath while raising the body. Bend the waist as much as possible. Crossing the legs is aimed at avoiding using the legs to support the body. Use the strength of the arms instead of the legs.

This exercise can regulate the *qi* of the lungs, promote the operation of the lung channels, and reinforce the function of the lungs.

2. Sit still. Relax the waist and back. Close the eyes

49

slightly. Make hollow fists and strike the middle and two sides of the back 5 times. When striking, hold breath. At the same time, clamp the teeth together 10 times, then slowly swallow saliva several times.

Points to remember: Strike the back in two directions: up-down and down-up. Strike the middle of the back first, then the sides.

This exercise can regulate and remove obstructions in the flow of *qi* in the lungs, promote normal operation of the channels and collaterals of the back, and prevent colds. It is good for the stomach and lungs.

3. Sit straight or stand. Raise the head and stretch the neck. Use the hands to rub the throat down to the chest. Repeat 20 times, using the hands alternately. Repeat the exercise 3 times without interruption.

Points to remember: Separate the thumb and the four fingers, press the part between the thumb and index finger on the throat and rub downward. Exert proper force.

This exercise is beneficial to the throat and can relieve cough and reduce phlegm.

4. Use the thumb to press the *tiantu* point 15 times. This can relieve cough and asthma.

5. Breathing exercise. Sit or stand in a place with fresh air. Breathe evenly. Inhale slowly through the nose. When the lungs are full, exhale slowly, at the same time pronouncing the sound "sh-h" gently. After exhaling all the air, inhale through the nose again. Repeat the exercise 24 to 36 times. Long practice of this exercise is effective for shortness of breath, cough and asthma. It can also reinforce the lungs and prevent colds.

Doing these exercises regularly in the autumn helps prevent colds, relieve coughing, reduce phlegm and strengthen the lungs. Of course, they can be done in other seasons as well. For those with chronic cough and asthma, these exercises help relieve pain and prevent recurrence.

Winter Exercises for Nourishing the Kidneys

YUAN LIREN

I N THE cold winter the ability of the metabolism of all living things becomes low. Aged and weak people feel the cold easily. Traditional Chinese medicine considers that this is caused by a shortage of the *yang* (heavenly) energy. *Yellow Emperor's Manual of Internal Medicine*, China's first medical literature, explains that the *yang* energy is like the sun which gives the earth light and heat. Without the sun all things on earth cannot live. Without *yang* energy, life will stop.

According to traditional Chinese medicine, *yang* energy is produced by the kidneys. The kidneys are the inborn source, the source of life and are in charge of the reproductive function. They are also the organs for the storage of nutrition cream. Whether one is in good or bad health fundamentally depends on whether the kidneys are strong or weak. When cold winter comes, the body needs enough energy and calories to ward off the cold. If one's kidneys are weak, the *yang* energy will also be weak, and one will suffer from dizziness, palpitations, shortness of breath, backache, even incontinence of the urine. Therefore, doing exercises for nourishing the kidneys not only prevents some diseases but improves health.

There are many traditional methods of nourishing the kidneys. In the winter, the days are short ad the nights long. Therefore go to bed a bit earlier and get up a bit later. Get much sun so that the body keeps warm. Eat high-calorie food. Don't wear tight clothing. Weak and aged people ought to eat

51

those foods that warm the kidneys, such as stewed mutton, thin-sliced instant-boiled mutton, chicken soup and duck. The following are exercises easy to do and helpful in nourishing the kidneys.

1. Sit up straight with legs apart as wide as the shoulders. Raise the hands slowly to the level of the ears with fingers pointing upward. Keep moving the hands up until they reach above the head. Then move them down to the original position. Repeat four times, and do this four times a day.

Points of attention: Relax before doing this. Breathe in when moving the hands up and out when moving them down. Do the movement gently. The exercise can limber the joints, stimulate the main and collateral channels and blood circulation, and make the vital energy gather at the *dantian* acupoint. It also helps relieve shortness of breath.

2. Sit up straight. Put left hand on left thigh. Bend right elbow with the palm upward and move it four times as if tossing something up in the air. Then do the same movement with left arm. Do the exercise four times a day.

Points of attention: Do the tossing movement quickly and breathe in. Breathe out when putting the hands on the thigh. The effects of this movement are the same as the first above.

3. Sit up straight with the legs hanging down naturally. Slowly turn torso left and right four times. Then swing the legs ten times depending on one's health.

Points of attention: Do this movement slowly and naturally with the body relaxed. Keep the torso straight while turning left and right. The movement helps nourish the kidneys and strengthen the back.

4. Sit up straight and untie the belt. Rub the hands together to warm them. Then put the palm on the back and rub up and down until you feel warm in the back. This movement warms the kidneys, strengthens the back, stimulates the circulation of blood and causes the muscles and joints to relax.

5. Keep the thighs tight together with the ankle bones touching each other. Cross the wrists on the breast, then raise

them above the head. Then bend over to touch the ground with the fingers. Squat down with arms embracing the knees, breathe out. Repeat ten times.

The above exercises are for nourishing the kidneys and the essence of life, strengthening vital energy, the back and the knees, and stimulating the main and collateral channels. They are considered beneficial to kidney and bladder-related diseases such as backache, weak knees, impotence, emission, vaginal discharge, deficiency of vital energy and dizziness.

No Sexual Intercourse in Drunkenness

ZHANG HUDE

A CCORDING to the *Yellow Emperor's Manual of Internal Medicine*, the earliest medical classic extant in China, one of the important causes limiting the longevity of humans is "sexual intercourse in drunkenness." The legendary Peng Zu, who is said to have enjoyed a long life, claimed that "sleeping alone is better than taking a hundred doses of life-preservation tonics."

Liquor has been popular since ancient times. Drinking a small amount can accelerate the circulation of the blood, reinforce the efficacy of medicine, improve the appetite and relieve fatigue. Traditional Chinese medicine uses liquor and medicinal ingredients to make medicinal liquors for treating diseases. Generally speaking, proper drinking is not opposed. But drinking too much, combined with sexual intercourse, means great harm to health. This is because while drunk people cannot control their behavior and sexual intercourse makes them overexcited. Indulgence in this greatly consumes the most fundamental substances in the body — *jing* and *qi*, the essence of life and vital energy.

T RADITIONAL Chinese medicine pays great attention to the role of sperm in men's health, considering it a key factor in preserving life. Luo Mingshan, 110, a traditional physician in Sichuan Province, said, "Sperm is a treasure of a man which should not be lost easily. Preserving it means preserving life, for in doing so a man can postpone the aging process." When asked the secret of his long life, he joked and said, "It is hard for you to learn my secret of living a hundred years, because I love the mountains and rivers much more than a beautiful wife." Modern immunology also proves that frequent sexual intercourse while drunk can retard the functions of the immunity system, cause excessive excitement, greatly consuming energy and reducing the adaptability of organs.

The ancients discussed the season and frequency of sexual intercourse. As to season, the *Inner Medicine* holds that "in winter sperm should be preserved." A medical expert named Zhu Danxi (1281-1358) of the Yuan Dynasty stressed that "in summer man should sleep alone." In terms of frequency, Sun Simiao of the Tang Dynasty said, "At the age of 20 men ejaculates once every four days; at 30 every eight days; at 40 every 16 days; at 50 every 21 days." Sperm grows from primitive reproductive cells, normally taking 60 days to mature. They are stored in the epididymis for 10 days before they possess reproductive capability. The seminal and prostate fluids also need time to accumulate. Reproduction capability reduces in the aging process, so older people need longer intervals. The frequency mentioned above basically conforms to physiological laws.

F ROM the angle of lengthening life, people should pay great attention to avoiding intercourse while drunk. It is not only harmful to their own health, but can seriously harm the next generation. Studies show that babies born of "intercourse in drunkenness" often suffer from mental disorders, hypertension, ulcers and other diseases. Elderly people are especially forbidden to make love while drunk because of weaknesses in vital energy and bodily functions.

Some doctors of traditional Chinese medicine hold that after the age of 60 men should stop sexual intercourse. Facts show that a controlled sexual life, later marriage and fewer offspring are indeed beneficial to health. Many emperors in Chinese history were short-lived because of their indulgence in liquor and women. On the other hand, a survey shows that 20 percent of the 72 centenarians in Sichuan Province controlled their sexual life and practiced family planning; 14 were married after the age of 40; 23 had only one child and 32 had no child at all.

That sexual intercourse while drunk harms health is also proved abroad. For example, a millionaire in Venice was on the edge of death at the age of 35 because of his indulgence in liquor and women. He adopted the advice of a doctor that he control his sexual life and drinking. He prolonged his life another half century. In his old age he wrote a book on his experience entitled *How to Live a Hundred Years*.

Life is precious, but it is also brief. For the happiness of yourself and your offspring, never make love in drunkenness.

Air Bath, Medicinal Bath and Dry Bath

LIU ZHANWEN

A IR baths, medicinal baths (water mixed with medicinal decoctions) and dry baths (rubbing the body with the palms) have a long history in China. With such bathing, people treat and prevent diseases and keep fit. They are simple and easy to do.

1. Air Bath

This is done to expose the naked body to cool air in order to raise the body temperature and thus regulate the functions of the central nerve system, increase the ability to endure cold, and activate the immunity system. A Chinese proverb says, "To keep fit, often stand in the cold."

Modern research proves that air bath can improve the functions of the inner systems and increase the content of a special substance in the blood which builds up one's resistance to disease. This is because fresh air contains large amounts of negative ions which can effectively regulate the central nerve system, improve the function of the cerebral cortex, promote metabolism, accelerate the process of oxidation and reduction, and increase immunity. According to reports in China and abroad, treating bronchial asthma patients by bathing them in negative ions gives a recovery rate of 80 percent.

Bathing in negative ions half an hour every day can reduce traffic accidents for drivers, raise study efficiency for students, and help athletes create good records. The air bath can help cure many chronic diseases such as bronchitis, asthma, tuberculosis, hepatitis, anemia and heart troubles. Frequent air baths can help patients recover sooner.

The air bath is simple and easy to do. It can be done anywhere at any time, and can be combined with manual labor and physical exercises. Generally speaking, it should be started in the summer. In the morning choose a place with fresh air to walk, jog, do morning exercises or *taijiquan*, wearing only vest and shorts. When autumn comes, wear as few clothes as possible and do more outdoor exercises. The duration of each bath can vary according to the weather and physical condition, as long as you do not shiver with the cold. Good ventilation should be kept in the room. Open a small window at night to left in fresh air. For elderly people the temperature of the room should not be lower than 15 degrees Centigrade. Fresh air and a temperature around 20 degrees is best.

2. Medicinal Bath

This is very old in China. Mix the water with a decoction

Winter swimming in Anshan City, northeast China.

of medicinal ingredients to wash or fume the body. This method was recorded over 2,000 years ago. Legends say that in the Zhou Dynasty (11th century-770 B. C.) bathing in "fragrant water" was very popular. A Qing Dynasty document also wrote that "bathing in water mixed with wolfberry decoction can prevent diseases and postpone the aging process." Medicinal baths can protect the skin, strengthen physique, treat and prevent diseases.

Different ingredients in the bath water have different functions. For example, a calamus decoction can protect the skin and make it smooth. To make it, boil 50 grams of calamus in water, then mix with bath water. Another method is to put the calamus directly in the bath tub and let it simmer in boiling water for 5 minutes. Take out the calamus, fill the tub with warm water and bathe.

The medicinal bath can treat and prevent many skin diseases such as nettle rash, geriatric dry skin, itching, as well as symptoms of rheumatic arthritis, chronic lumbar pain and backache, anal ailments, eye diseases and mycosis. Better results can be obtained under the guidance of doctors.

A decoction of Chinese mugwort and chrysanthemum mixed in the bath water is effective for eczema. Boil 50 grams of mugwort and chrysanthemum and mix with bath water. For rheumatic arthritis, chronic lumbar pain and leg pain, the following ingredients are required: 30 grams of mulberry twigs, 15 grams of cassic twigs, 15 grams of cuidium officiuale, 10 grams of reticulate millettia, 10 grams each of safflower, sapanwood, angelica, ground beetle, large-leaved gentian, slender acanthopanaz skin, the root of Chinese clematis, frankincense and myrrh. This prescription can stimulate the circulation of the blood, relax muscles and joints, remove stasis in the blood and relieve pain.

To treat swollen eyes, boil 10 grams of rhizome of Chinese goldthread, 10 grams of cape jasmine, and 10 grams of root of large-flowered skullcap into a decoction. Fume and wash the eyes while it is hot. This can relieve swelling and pain.

3. Dry Bath

This is rubbing the skin of the entire body with the two hands. The process can regulate the *qi* and blood flow, protect the skin, and coordinate the functions of the inner organs. Modern research proves that stimulating the nerve endings by rubbing the skin can accelerate the circulation of blood and lymph, promote metabolism, increase immunity, and postpone the aging process.

It can be done in two ways. First, rub the two hands together until they feel hot, then rub the arms, then from head to feet. The second is to start from the top of the head (the *baihui* point), to the face, shoulders and arms, chest, abdomen, waist and back, then to the legs, ending at the *yongquan* point at the center of the arch of the foot.

The best time for a dry bath is in the evening before going to bed and in the morning on awakening. The temperature of the room should be proper (22 degrees Centigrade) and the ventilation good. Go to the lavatory before rubbing. Remove clothing. Take a sitting position or lie on the bed.

A simpler method is to use a dry towel to rub the skin, or use a soft brush for what is called a "brush bath." Regular dry bathing will make the skin smooth and soft. Do not use too much force to avoid damaging the skin. As long as one practices persistently, one can prevent disease and keep fit.

Point to remember: those with acute infections, contagious diseases, tuberculosis, hemophilia, purpura caused by reduced platelets, and open wounds should not have a dry bath.

There are other forms of baths that can be adopted according to local conditions, such as warm water bath, hot water bath, cold water bath, hot spring bath, steam bath, sea water bath, sunbath, sand bath, mud bath, etc.

Sleeping Well — the Key to a Long Life

ZHANG HUDE

ABOUT one third of our life is spent sleeping with our head on the pillow. Sleep and good health is a life-long companion. Traditional Chinese medicine constantly stresses the scientific nature of sleep. "Sleep and eating are the keys to preserving health." "Those who sleep well can eat well and live long." After five years of investigation and study of 7,000 people, two American scientists reached the conclusion that there are seven factors that influence life expectancy, and one of these is good sleep. What can be called good sleep? There are 11 points:

1. Getting up and going to bed should be regular. Based on the theory that "heaven is interrelated with humans," traditional Chinese medicine maintains that we should arrange our life in regular patterns according to the different seasons. For example, in the spring "go to sleep late, arise early and take a walk in the yard." In the summer, "go to sleep late, arise early and you'll not feel weary during the day." In the autumn "go to sleep early, arise early together with the rooster." And in the winter "go to sleep early, arise late with the sun." That is to say, in spring and summer sleep can be shortened; while in autumn and winter sleep can be more. In short, changing your time for sleep casually now and then is likely to disturb the life system and damage your spirit, causing either poor sleep or an addiction to too much sleep. Elderly people especially should work and rest according to the rhythm of their biological clock,

Singing Peking Opera in a park.

which is difficult to change.

2. Sleeping time. This varies from person to person and from time to time. Therefore, no uniformity should be imposed. Eight hours is the usual average. People of different ages need different times, however. For example, babies under one need 14 to 18 hours; a juvenile between 7 and 15 needs 10 hours; an adult needs 8 hours; people 60 to 70 need 7 to 8 hours, those 70 to 80 need 6 to 7 hours, and those 80 to 90 need 9 to 10 hours. The Research Center for Sleep Studies of Stanford University found that sleep is related to many factors such as the periodic fluctuations of body temperature, the state of one's health, the intensity of work, nutrition, and work conditions (factors such as high temperatures and noise). When your health is not good, you need more sleep than usual.

Sleep time is also related to one's character. A lively, sanguine disposition usually does not need 8 hours sleep, while a quiet, sentimental character needs 9 to 10 hours.

Of course, good sleep depends not only on the length of time, but on the quality of the sleep. The criterion for good sleep is that it should recover one's spirit and physical strength. As long as you get rid of fatigue, are comfortable, think clearly and are energetic and competent in the work of the day, it is sufficient sleep no matter how little you had.

3. The environment for sleep. Air conditioners are an important factor in improving the sleep environment, but people have become aware of their deficiencies. Traditional ways of keeping the air in the bedroom fresh are still not out-of-date. Open your window in the daytime to bring in plenty of oxygen. In temperate seasons such as spring, summer and autumn, you can sleep with the window open, though the breeze should not blow directly on your face, for it is cooler than the room temperature. In badly ventilated rooms in the cities, the carbon dioxide in the air is as high as 30 times more than in the countryside. Sleeping in such a condition is likely to give nightmares and when awakening headache and a feeling of dizziness and weakness.

If the room is not ventilated, there is likely to be a big difference between in-room and out-of-room temperatures and this might cause colds. In the winter, open a small transom to ensure air circulation. Room temperature should be kept between 18° C and 20° C. Too warm or too cold will influence sleep; so will a strong light, noise, unpleasant neighbors, etc., while a quiet, clean and comfortable environment makes it easier to fall asleep. If there is noise, do as Tao Yuanming, an ancient Chinese poet, said, "Living in a noisy town, you won't feel it if you don't care."

4. Sleeping position. Many people do not care about this. But if your position is not correct, it may not only affect your sleep but harm your health. For instance, some people like to sleep on their stomach, but they never thought that such a position presses their chest and stomach, hinders breathing and decreases vital capacity. It also presses the heart and interferes with its functions. Some people like to sleep on their left side, but this also presses their heart and sometimes causes nightmares. Some people like to sleep on the back, unconsciously putting their hands on their chest, stretching the legs out. This can stretch the muscles too tightly and disturb rest.

The right posture for good sleep should be to lie on your

right side. Bend the legs slightly, relax the body, put one hand with arm bend before your pillow, the other on your thigh. The backbone is bow-shaped, the legs and arms can move easily and the muscles of the whole body are relaxed. This helps muscle tissues get enough rest and removes fatigue. Meanwhile, sleeping on your right side puts your heart in a high position, helping it to drain blood and release its burden. The liver can obtain more blood, for it is in a low position. It also helps the stomach move food to the duodenum. A lot of old people sum this all up with "Sit like sitting, sleep like sleeping, go to sleep like the crescent moon." This makes sense.

5. What you sleep with. First, the height of the pillow should be moderate. There is a saying, "Shake up the pillow and have a good sleep," but shake the pillow doesn't mean that the higher it is, the better. Usually 8 to 15 cm is preferred because your head can bend a little forward, your neck muscles can be fully relaxed, breathing can be free, and the blood supply to the brain normal. The pillow should be neither too hard nor too soft, and should have some elasticity.

The medical pillow should be mentioned. In ancient times, those who wanted to preserve good health liked to use a medical pillow. This not only made sleep comfortable but prevented and cured disease, for instance, people with hypertension used a pillow filled with mung bean or silkworm residue. This has an anti-pyretic effect, gives clear sight and can eliminate headache. Those with neurasthenia used a "pillow with mgnetite."

Second, the bed should not be too hard or too soft, for a hard bed cannot meet the needs of the curved body and can cause reflected pressure on the cervical vertebrae. If the bed is too soft, the middle part of the body will sink, curving the trunk and adding a burden to the ligaments and joints of the cervical vertebrae. A wooden bed with strung crisscrossed coir ropes is soft and springy, yet retains enough hardness.

If you are accustomed to sleep naked, you should wear soft, loose pajamas instead of close-fitting underwear, thus allowing the blood of the skin to circulate properly.

6. Good sleep first of all requires that you relax the heart. "First relax the heart" means that before falling asleep your nerves should not be excited. Traditional Chinese medicine believes that people fall asleep easily when mentally quiet. If you are excited, nervous or too concentrated on something, it is difficult to fall asleep. Therefore, before going to bed you should not read books or magazines, especially literature and art, for they can make thoughts throng your mind and you become anxious. You should not talk volubly with your friends in order not to become excited, anxious or vexed. In short, "only when the masculine air enters the feminine side can you get to sleep," only after your heart is relaxed. Before you sleep, dispel distracting thoughts and put your mind on sleep.

7. Cultivate good sleep habits. Before going to sleep, brushing your teeth and washing your feet is a good habit. Washing your feet in warm water not only cleans them but is a good stimulus to your mind. Drinking alcohol, tea or coffee, eating chocolate or smoking are not good habits. When in bed, do not tuck your head under the blanket.

8. Diet moderately. Traditional Chinese medicine thinks that "if the stomach is not comfortable, sleep is not peaceful." If you eat too much before going to sleep, your stomach and intestines will have too much to do. Yet if you go to sleep too late, you may not fall asleep because of hunger.

9. Don't sleep too much. Traditional Chinese medicine holds that "sleeping too much hurts the vital energy" and influences its flow, possibly leading to dizziness, weakness of the limbs and a jaded appetite.

10. Work and rest moderately. Violent sports, physical labor or intense mental work excites the nerves. So before going to sleep do not overwork. But "fatigue is the best sleeping pill." If you work or study hard during the day, tiredness in the evening will make it easy to fall asleep. After retirement, elderly people usually do less mental and physical work, and therefore are not able to work and rest moderately, which

leads to restless sleep. To compensate, do some work during the day, or take a 30-minute walk before going to bed.

11. Treat insomnia actively. Insomnia is a bitter thing. When night falls, heavyheartedness and worry comes. The more one worries, the more difficult it is to fall asleep. This becomes a vicious circle. To treat insomnia, first try to find the real cause. If it is because of habits bad for sleep, such as drinking strong tea or playing cards or chess before bedtime, change it. If it is caused by the sleep environment, such as temperature too high or too low, change these factors too. If it is caused by disease, for example neurasthenia, get proper treatment. Do not neglect insomnia.

Clothing and Heath

LIU ZHANWEN

C LOTHES, symbol of civilization, should first protect the body from heat and cold, injury and being invaded by disease. Second, they reflect the outlook, living standard and age of people. Artistic and tasteful clothes make a person look noble and dignified.

But people should not just pay attention to style, they should also make sure that clothes are comfortable and good for health. Whatever their design, pattern and style, they should be warm and fit well. Room must be left between the body and the clothing for exchange of heat, which gives the feeling of comfort. Researchers believe that if the climate inside clothing remains at $32° \pm 1°C$ in temperature, $50° \pm 10\%$ in humidity, and 25 ± 15 cm/sec. air exchange, the body temperature will be normal. Only normal temperature can help improve the efficiency of work and the speed of recovery from illness.

From the point of view of health and longevity, comfort in clothing is the prime need. Thus, the selection of material and design are very important. Patterns must vary with the season, place and person.

Clothes for Spring

In the spring, the *yang* (heavenly energy) rises and the climate is changeable. Specialists in the maintenance of good health believe that much attention should be paid to wind and coldness. Clothes for spring should be loose, soft and warm. Cotton is ideal for underclothes because it absorbs well, has good ventilation and retains heat. Though dacron is thin, it does not do these well. Early spring often brings sudden

In Shanghai, light movement sports are organized for senior citizens.

A Fujian Province folk instruments orchestra.

changes in temperatures. For fitness, clothing should not be reduced too early, or it becomes easier to catch colds or other illnesses. Clothes should be increased or reduced according to temperature changes, thus helping the body to get used to the climate of spring.

Clothes for Summer

To take account of the heat, summer clothes must have good ventilation to let body heat out, allowing absorption and evaporation. They should be of light, soft material and of light colors that reflect radiation. Best materials for this are linen and pure silk. These are light, ventilate well and are comfortable as underwear. Pure cotton absorbs well but does not let body heat out as well. Cotton underwear often sticks to the body because of sweat. Thus neither cotton nor dacron is good for summer dress or underwear. The patterns for summer dress should be lively and of much variety, such as vests, T-shirts, shorts, shirts and pants. Skirts and dresses for girls and women should be light, cool and graceful.

Autumn Clothes

As the temperatures go down slowly, the changes are not so abrupt as in the spring, neither are they stable. An old saying goes, "There are four seasons in a day and the weather differs in only 10 *li* (5 km)." To be sure of staying warm, more clothes should be prepared — lined jackets, sweat shirts, thin sweaters, light overcoats. Clothes should be added steadily as the cold increases, thus preparing the body for freezing winter. Add them gradually, for putting all on at once does not build up adaptability and also restricts activity. This is why we often say, "Don't take off clothes in the spring until the weather becomes really warm, and in the autumn don't put on clothes until the weather becomes really cool."

Winter Clothes

Material for winter clothes should be good heat conductors and preservers, such as wool, polyvinyl and other synthetic fibers such as orlon. Dark colors are better heat absorbers. In winter the *yang* should be kept. Cotton underwear is warm and comfortable in winter. Coats, shoes and socks should be relatively big and loose to provide good circulation of vital energy and blood, warming arms and legs.

With fur or sweat clothes, the fur side and soft nap should face inside, for they store a large quantity of air which acts as an insulation and prevents the loss of body heat. This is why people wear woolen knitwear. Cotton is now replaced with soft, light and warm silk floss, camel hair, artificial wool and down. But to wear excessively warm clothing will cause the loss of *yang* and this, in the following spring, will cause colds and other illnesses.

Clothes should not only be changed with the seasons but with each change of temperature within the season. This im-

Proves metabolism, strengthens resistance to disease and helps prolong life.

Clothing should be changed and washed regularly but the following taboos must be remembered.

1. Don't take clothes off while you are sweating. Ancient health specialists pointed out that skin texture and hair follicles are open when sweating. Colds come easily if you change clothes at this time.

2. After the sweating ceases, change to clean and dry clothes at once. Sun Simiao, ancient health specialist, said, "One should not wear wet or sweated clothes long, for this may cause skin ulcers or itching." Clothes drenched with sweat dry slowly, making the body lose a large quantity of *yang*. Skin weakly defended and humid can lead to pathological changes such as rheumatism.

3. Clothes should not be too tight. Fashion rather than health often dictates the selection of clothes. Some patterns, such as jeans and tight-fitting outfits, may be popular but do not give enough attention to health, affecting normal circulation of vital energy and blood and even breathing. Those under 18 years, girls in particular, should not wear tight clothes. Neither should those with dermatitis, carbuncles, piles and urethritis, those who sweat a lot, pregnant women, and those with chronic diseases such as TB and diabetes. Fashion designers should not only pay attention to style but to the effect of their clothes on health.

How to Keep Your Hair in Good Condition

LIU ZHANWEN

HAIR and skin are the mirrors of one's health. People with nice hair look energetic and healthy. Some people with white, thin or varicolored hair, or baldness are disconsolate. Whether the hair is healthy or withered is connected with general health. Traditional Chinese medicine believes that the hair has close relations with the kidneys, liver, heart, lungs and brain. Dark, sleek, soft and fast-growing hair is evidences of energy, a body full of vital energy and blood, and a healthy brain. Sparse or white hair indicates disease and decrepitude. An old saying goes like this: "A person gets old first in the hair."

Hair is not only an indicator of health, its elasticity and toughness also protects the head and brain, and it has the function of metabolism. This is why people want beautiful hair. The following instructions can achieve results:

1. Comb and massage the hair regularly. Ancient specialists in health held that hair should be combed frequently. This should not be merely regarded as beautifying yourself; it is important to prevent aging and disease. A Chinese book on the causes of various diseases says, "Hair will not turn white if it is combed regularly." Another on longevity says, "Frequent combing improves the eyesight and relieves colds. The hair should be combed 120 times." It is best to comb it three times a day, morning, noon and before going to bed. Comb backward from the forehead, forward from the back of the head, and

then comb it from left to right and right to left, 45 times. Fingers can play the same role. Massage your head softly with your fingers, first from forehead to the top of the head, then downward to the back, from the temples to the top of the head 10 times. After massage the scalp will feel hot and tight.

Medical research has pointed out that regular combing or massage has the following five effects: (1) it smoothes arteries and veins; (2) improves the circulation of the blood in the head; (3) nourishes the hair and prevents loss; (4) improves the eyesight, improves health and helps prevent cerebral hemorrhage; and (5) invigorates the function of the brain, refreshes the body and relieves fatigue.

2. Wash the hair frequently. Cao Cishan, health specialist in the Qing Dynasty, wrote in a medical book, "Hair should be combed but not washed regularly. One will get a cold if it is washed in a wind." The ancients believed that the elderly and weak should wash their hair less often than people in good health. It is hygienically necessary to wash the hair. Since the sebaceous glands secrete a large quantity of esters, which not only keeps the hair supple but is bacterostatic, excessive washing or washing with ordinary soap will remove this protector of the hair and shorten its life. Serious overwashing may lead to ringworm.

Generally speaking, dry hair should be washed once every 10 to 15 days. If it is not so dry, once a week is good. Greasy hair should be washed every five days. The water should not be too hot but about 37℃. Hot water is harmful because it tends to turn the hair dry and fragile. But if the water is too cold, it doesn't wash clean. Different shampoos should be used for different types of hair. Neutral or dry hair should use toilet soap or neutral shampoo, greasy hair should use ordinary soap or laundry soap, or a shampoo containing more alkaline. Babies' hair should be washed with a special baby soap because their skin is very delicate.

Having your hair done can keep your hair in style, but almost every solution used contains sodium bicarbonate and ammonia which will damage your hair to some degree. Moreover, permed hair will turn yellow, fragile and lose its gloss. So hair should not be done with chemicals more than once in 5 months, even longer if the hair is normally dry. Children and those who are weak, allergic to chemicals, pregnant or lying in should not have their hair done with chemicals.

3. Be pleasant. Traditional Chinese medicine believes that the mental factor has much to do with changes in the condition of the hair. The hair will turn white or fall if one is narrow-minded, burdened with anxiety or mentally too tired. An old Chinese saying goes like this: "Laugh once and be ten years younger, but worry will turn your hair white." It is said that in the Spring and Autumn Period (770-467 B.C.) Wu Zixu fled from the State of Chu to the State of Wu. As he traveled, he came to Zhaoguan Pass where he knew he might be arrested. He was so nervous that his hair and beard turned white overnight. He escaped the following day because this had changed him beyond recognition. The story exaggerates but tells us that hair condition has a close relation with spirit. Therefore, people should try to refrain from being upset, train a strong will, stay broad-minded, optimistic and calm in order to meet the complications of life. This can not only keep your hair in good condition but is conducive to good physical and mental health.

4. Take care of your hair. Those who work in strong sunshine or dusty places should wear caps. But caps should not be so tight that they affect sweat drainage. On rainy days the hair should be protected. The hair should not become muggy, so caps should not be worn a long time. If your work requires a cap, safety helmets with ventilation help ensure healthy hair growth.

5. Pay attention to diet. A variety of diets that keep a balance between acid and base helps prevent baldness and white hair. Eat foods containing proper protein, iodine, calcium and vitamins B, A and E such as in milk, fish, eggs, coarse grain, green vegetables, fruit, especially melons. Those with gray,

dry and thin hair should take Chinese medicine for prevention and treatment. Those whose hair has fallen or turned white early for their age because of physical weakness should eat walnuts and take *Shouwu Yanshou Dan* and the tonic *Qi Bao Mei Xu Dan* to build up the kidneys.

Very important for beautiful, health hair: Give up smoking, drinking and over-eating. Do physical training regularly, strike a proper balance between work and rest, use your brain rationally and live a regular life with good habits and customs.

Chinese Medicine and Dental Hygiene

LIU ZHANWEN

DURING an average lifetime, a person consumes roughly 40 tons of food. The processing of this enormous quantity of material begins, of course, in the mouth. How well the teeth perform their grinding and chewing function will inevitably have an effect on the whole body. For this reason, dental and mouth hygiene have always held an important place in Chinese medical theories on health and longevity.

Two thousand years ago there was already a saying that advised: "The first thing in the morning, wash the face and rinse the mouth." Over a thousand years ago, the Chinese people were using bone tooth brushes.

In Chinese medicine an important role is given to the saliva, which is considered a precious fluid. This comes from the theory of the Fluids of the Five Organs. Perspiration is the heart fluid, nasal mucus is the lung fluid, tears are the liver fluid, and saliva is the fluid of the spleen and the kidneys. Since the latter two organs are vital for a long, healthy life, saliva too becomes especially precious. Classic medical authorities prescribed: "Frequently press the tongue against the teeth, collect the saliva and swallow it. Let it lubricate the five internal organs and enliven the skin. Such is the way to long life."

Modern science has indeed shown that saliva has many properties: it aids digestion, neutralizes gastric acids, helps repair intestinal membranes, and is a mild antiseptic. Saliva also bathes the teeth, washing out food and thus protecting them.

A Uygur centenarian feeding ducks.

Saliva contains calcium, sodium, chlorine, ammonia, oxygen, nitrogen, carbon dioxide, proteins, and amino acids. These substances all enhance metabolism, growth and the body's immunity system. Hormones of the salivary glands delay the aging process. Saliva also seems to have an inhibiting effect on carcinogenic substances. Clearly, any methods that will improve mouth hygiene will have a salutary effect on the whole body.

The following are some of the more important parts of dental hygiene from Chinese medicine:

1. Frequent clamping of the teeth together. This strengthens the teeth so that they do not fall out with age. Most people who live to an old age usually retain a fair number of healthy teeth. This exercise should be done in the morning and evening. The method is to be calm, relaxed and lightly close the lips. First clamp the molars together 50 times, then the incisors 50 times. Then slightly move the lower jaw to one side so the canines can clamp together, also 50 times. The numbers of clenches and the frequency can, of course, be increased.

2. Rinsing and swallowing saliva. This can often be done after the tooth clamping. Move the tongue gently around the teeth, left and right, up and down, along the inner and outer surfaces, in all 30 times. As the saliva increases, push it toward the upper palate with the tongue. When a sufficient quantity has collected, puff the cheeks and rinse the mouth ten times with the saliva, then swallow it in three deep gulps, as if sending it down below the navel. This is a very simple exercise which can be carried out anywhere at any time. If done frequently, it can help prevent toothaches and sore throats. It also increases the appetite and aids digestion.

3. Brushing the teeth morning and night. The night brushing is particularly important, for the secretion of saliva is least during the night and its natural washing effect is at a minimum. Brushing should be up-and-down, not sideways which not only does not get rid of particles of food between the teeth but can also damage tooth surfaces. Elderly people should use soft brushes. False teeth should be taken out and washed every

night.

4. Frequent rinsing of the mouth. This should be done after every meal, and particularly after eating sweet things. In China, people rinse with water and tea. In the old days, cold water was most popular. For tea rinsing, the tea should be strong. This helps rid the mouth of grease and freshens the breath. Tea contains fluorine which strengthens the teeth.

5. Correct chewing. Food should be chewed and swallowed slowly so as to thoroughly mix it with the saliva. The teeth on both sides of the mouth should be used. Habitually chewing on one side can only cause atrophy of the unused side and lead to tooth and gum problems. It can also lead to oversensitivity of the teeth or inflammation. In extreme cases the face may even become lop-sided.

6. Massage of the lips. The method is to close the lips and use the ring finger of either hand to gently massage the lips until there is a hot sensation. This stimulates blood circulation in the mouth and gums, and increases their resistance to disease and infection.

7. Proper nutrition. Vitamins A, C, D and the B group as well as calcium, phosphorous and proteins are all essential to the proper development of healthy teeth. Fruit, vegetables and animal products which contain these substances should be eaten regularly. Pregnant and nursing mothers, babies and young children should pay special attention to their diet.

8. The use of medicines. The imperial archives of the Qing Dynasty (1644-1911) contain a secret prescription for protecting the teeth. It was made of 12 major ingredients and was applied to the gums every morning. It was particularly effective against toothache caused by digestive problems.

9. The avoidance of bad habits. The use of toothpicks can cause damage to the gums and lead to infection and sores. Children should not suck pencils and other dangerous items.

10. Prevention. Pregnant and nursing mothers as well as young children should not take tetracycline in large doses or for long periods, as this can lead to permanent staining of the tooth

enamel and other disorders. Poor alignment of the teeth in children should be corrected, preferably between the ages of 13 and 15. Everyone should have regular dental checkups.

All these methods are simple yet can bring great benefits to those who practice them regularly.

Foot Rubbing Exercise

YUAN LIREN

A MONG the traditional Chinese exercises, those for the foot occupy an important place. Without feet man cannot stand, walk, run or jump, and the movements of the feet show whether a man is healthy. So medical experts down through the ages have summed up many effective exercises to keep the feet fit. Rubbing the arch of the foot is one of them. It is simple and easy to practice.

Su Dongpo (1037-1101) of the Song Dynasty was not only a great scholar but also a researcher on ways to keep fit. He told his contemporaries that one measure for keeping fit was rubbing the arches of the feet. He said, "I have paid great attention to methods of keeping fit. I choose easy ones to practice and do them regularly. Since I am now idle, I use the time to do research, and have realized that attaining longevity is not unfounded. In the beginning I could not see the result. After three months of practice, however, I found its effect was a hundred times better than taking medicine. Its miraculous effect I cannot describe in languages."

The key spot to be rubbed is the *yongquan* point at the center of the arch at the bottom of the foot. This point is on the kidney channel, which starts from the little toe, crosses the center of the arch to the ankle, through the legs to the spinal cord, then from the abdomen to the chest, finally ending at the throat and tongue. Regular rubbing of *yongquan* point stimulates the circulation of the blood and *qi*, and causes the muscles and joints to relax. When the *qi* and blood flourish, they nourish the whole body, making the legs and waist strong, strengthening the kidneys, raising resistance to diseases and

81

postponing the aging process. Rubbing the arch of the foot can also treat *yin* deficiency (insufficiency of body fluid, with irritability, thirst, constipation as symptoms), relieve internal heat and soothe nerves. It is also effective in ailments of the head, eyes, throat, digestive organs, and for relieving the symptoms of fever, vomiting, dysentery and neurasthenia.

This exercise is easy to do. Chen Zhi of the Song Dynasty (960-1279) wrote a book entitled *Keeping Fit in Old Age*. One chapter described the exercise in detail: "The *yongquan* point is located at the center of the arch, from which dampness intrudes. In the daytime or at night, I often rub the arches of my feet alternately. Use one hand to hold the toes, and the other to rub. After a while I feel the arch warm, then turn my toes a bit. If I feel tired, I rest for a moment. Asking someone else to rub is all right. But self-rubbing is much better." Chen Zhi did this exercise regularly, "often rubbing thousands of tims."

Proceed as follows:

1. Dry rubbing. Put the two feet opposite, sole upward. Use one hand to hold the toes, and the thumb of the other to rub the *yongquan* point 90 times without interruption. Moving back and forth is counted as one time. Count the number of rubbings precisely. At the beginning, rub 30 times. After a time, increase to 60, then 90. The finger can be used to press the *yongquan* point to increase the effect. Persistence in foot rubbing reinforces the brain, benefits the kidneys, and strengthens the legs and entire body.

Points to remember: Don't use so much force that you feel pain and discomfort. Do it morning and evening.

2. Wet rubbing. Fill a basin with warm water (about 38° C.), put the feet into the basin and soak ankle-deep for a while. When the feet become red, use the left hand to hold the left foot and the right hand to hold the right foot, the two arches opposite each other. Use the thumbs to rub the *yongquan* points 90 times without interruption. This soothes the nerves, invigorates the circulation of the blood, and is effective in treating insomnia, and dream-disturbed sleep.

To treat indigestion, jaded appetite, constipation, diarrhea and abdominal distension, enlarge the sphere of rubbing. Adults can help children massage the arches.

This exercise is not limited by environment or location, and can be done in morning and evening. Persistence will yield good results. This is the reason it has been handed down from generation to generation.

'Light Labor' Exercise

YUAN LIREN

T RADITIONAL Chinese exercises include not only sophis-
ticated routines but many simple, easy ones. "Light labor"
is one of them.

As its name indicates, "light labor" means exercises requiring light movements. The principle is to act within one's
capability and never overreach. Sun Simiao, a great Tang Dynasty physician a thousand years ago, said, "To keep fit, regular exercise is necessary, but never overreach oneself." Excessive exercises do not strengthen physique but on the contrary,
harm health. Proper exercises accelerate the circulation of the
blood, limber the joints, aid digestion, coordinate the functions of the inner organs and increase metabolism.

"Light labor" exercises can be practiced in two ways: during household chores and in athletic exercises.

1. Household chores. Cao Tingdong of the Qing Dynasty
wrote that "elderly people should regularly attend household
chores requiring light strength such as dusting the table, washing the inkslab, burning incense, boiling water for tea, filling
flower vases, rolling up the curtain, and so on. Light labor
makes the blood flow more quickly. Just as an old saying says,
'Running water is never stale and a door hinge never gets
worm-eaten,' so regular movements make one strong."

This method is applicable for weak, ill and elderly people.
Exercising while attending to light household chores will make
old people's lives more interesting, colorful and rhythmical.

2. Athletic exercises. This form involves four parts of the
body. Pu Qianguan of the Song Dynasty wrote in his *Outlines
of Life Preservation*, "If a man wants to prolong his life, he

should practice 'light labor' exercises to accelerate the circulation of the blood. When sitting, never sit too long; when walking, never walk too fast to avoid overtiredness. This is the principle of 'light labor' exercises."

Proceed as follows:

(1) Exercise of the arms: Drawing a bow, weightlifting, fist striking and arm swinging.

Drawing a bow. Sit straight or stand with the knees bending and the feet apart. Exert force on the two arms as if drawing a bow, but don't exert too much force. Repeat 10 times, using the left and right arm alternately. One can increase or decrease the number of actions according to the condition of one's health.

Weightlifting. Raise the arms above the head, palms upward. Stretch and bend the arms as if lifting a heavy stone. Repeat 15 times.

Fist striking. Make hollow fists, strike forward with the left and right fist alternately. Repeat 10 times.

Arm swinging. Let the arms hang naturally, then swing them gently forward and backward. Repeat 15 times.

(2) Exercise of the head. Relax the neck, then raise head, lower it, and turn it right and left.

(3) Exercise of the waist. Turn the waist left and right, then bend it forward and backward. Repeat 5 times.

(4) Exercise of the hand.

Hand rubbing. Clasp the hands together and rub them as if washing them. Repeat 10 times.

Face rubbing. First rub the hands. When they feel warm, cover the eyes with the two palms. A moment later, rub the face with the palms as if washing it. Repeat 10 times or until the face feels slightly warm.

"Light labor" exercises limber the arms and legs, head, neck and waist. Traditional Chinese medicine holds that the four limbs are the stems of the *yang* (positive) channels. The bending, stretching and rubbing of the limbs promotes the flow of the *qi* (vital energy) in the channels and collaterals, which are closely connected with the digestive system. Exercise of the limbs reinforces the spleen and stomach, and helps digestion. Using the palms to cover the eyes benefits the liver and improves eyesight. Face rubbing helps prevent colds. Regular rubbing of the face raises resistance to colds and makes the complexion rosy and lustrous. Exercises of the neck and waist limber the joints.

"Light labor" exercises can be done anywhere at any time. It is suitable for middle-aged and old people of both sexes. Again, persistence will result in keeping fit.

'Contradictory Force' Exercises for Sedentary Workers

YUAN LIREN

S UCH exercises limber arm and leg muscles and joints, promote the normal function of channels and collaterals, invigorate the circulation of the blood and qi, and thus aid in preventing and treating diseases. This form of exercises was recorded in medical documents as early as the Song Dynasty (960-1279). The principle involves the use of opposing strengths.

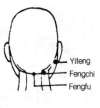

Yifeng
Fengchi
Fengfu

Fig. 1

Proceed as follows:

1. Exercise of the head and arms. Sit straight. Clasp hands. Put them on the back of the neck. Raise the head and turn it left and right. Exert strength when raising and turning the head. At the same time, exert contradictory forces between hands and neck. Repeat 5 times (Fig. 1).

On the back of the neck are the *fengchi*, *fengfu* and *yifeng* points. When the hands on the back of the neck are exerting force, these points are massaged. At the same time the muscles and joints of the neck and arms are limbered. This exercise regulates the *qi* and blood flow, helps prevent colds, clears the mind, improves eyesight and relieves headaches.

2. Exercise of arms, legs, shoulders and back. Sit on a chair. Bend the body forward, using the left hand to pull the left foot, putting the thumb on the *taichong* point (Fig. 2). Straighten the waist, pull the foot upward and stretch the leg. Exert enough force on the hand, foot, leg and waist, the whole body tightening like a drawn bow. Then change to the right hand and right foot and do the same. Repeat 4 times.

The process looks simple but much force is required to tighten the body like a bow. Hold the breath while doing the

Fig. 2

exercise. This exercise limbers all the joints. It helps relieve pain and spasm in waist and legs. For weak, ill and elderly people, it strengthens the physique and makes the limbs stronger. Massage of the *taichong* points improves eyesight, soothes nerves and regulates the functions of the liver and kidneys. It can also alleviate dizziness and hypertension.

"Contradictory force" exercises are simple, easy to do and can be done anywhere at any time. Practice three times every day. Persistance gives good results.

Exercises for Shoulders, Elbows, Waist and Knees

YUAN LIREN

E LDERLY people often feel weak in their limbs and pain in their joints, especially in the shoulders, elbows, lumbar and knees, making work and life difficult. Traditional Chinese medicine holds that these symptoms are caused by an inadequate supply of nourishment to these joints due to weak functioning of the vital energy and blood circulation. Proper movements will improve these and relieve the pain. Doctors often hear patients say, "I feel pain all over my body. Some movements make me feel better." Some traditional Chinese exercises are good for these joints. Here are three of them:

1. "Black dragon stretches its claws"

Stand straight with the feet close to each other. Make fists. Raise them as high as the breasts. Exert force on the fists as you press the chest, but not too hard.

(1) Turn the upper body left, loosen the right fist, palm upward, with the fingers close together. Stretch the right arm left forward, eyes following the palm, counting to 30 with the rhythm of the breath.

(2) Turn the right palm downward. With the right arm draw a curve downward while bending at the waist. When the palm passes the knee, stretch the arm sideways. Do this movement fast.

(3) Straighten the waist, put the right hand back to the right breast as in the starting position.

Then change to the left hand and do the same. Repeat 15 times on each hand. Then stand straight, relax the body, breathe evenly, with the arms hanging down naturally. This exercise is for pain in the shoulders, elbows and waist (Fig. 1).

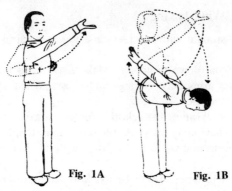

Fig. 1A   Fig. 1B

2. "Separate the white horse's mane"

Separate the legs and squat a little with the feet apart. Let the arms hang naturally.

(1) Bend the waist forward. Stretch the two arms downward as if embracing something in your arms. Cross the two hands before the knees (Fig. 2).

(2) Straighten the waist. Raise the arms, cross the wrists

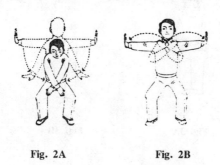

Fig. 2A   Fig. 2B

in front of the face with palms toward the face. Turn the palms outward, separate the arms and stretch them horizontally.

Repeat this 5 times. Those with shoulder and lumbar pain can do this exercise regularly.

3. "Wind boxing"

Stand straight with the feet close together, arms hanging naturally.

(1) Squat down promptly. Make fists. Bend the elbows and put the arms between legs and chest. When squatting, don't raise the heels.

(2) Following the elastic force caused by prompt squatting, stand up quickly. At the same time stretch the arms sideways horizontally. Turn the fists, with the hollow downward.

Repeat 15 times. Don't be too fast. The speed of movements should be according to the condition of your health. This exercise is applicable to those with pains in shoulders, elbows, waist and knees.

These exercises are simple and easy to learn. Practicing 3 times daily helps treat ailments in shoulders, elbows, waist and knees. Long-time practice strengthens the physique.

Fig. 3A   Fig. 3B

Lying Exercises to Postpone the Aging Process

YUAN LIREN

MOST elderly people feel weak both mentally and physically, their abilities fall short of their wishes. They sleep less and awake easily, are slow in thought, have a failing memory and a poor appetite, and cannot stand cold. Their limbs are not so dexterous, and sometimes they feel pain all over the body and numbness in parts. These are all normal indications of the aging process.

Traditional Chinese medicine holds that movements strengthen physique. Regular exercises invigorate the circulation of *qi* and the blood, accelerate the metabolism, eliminate various disorders, postpone the aging process and keep exuberant vitality.

Among the traditional Chinese exercises, many are suitable for elderly people. A book entitled *Essays on Preserving Life* described a set of "lying exercises."

Proceed as follows:

1. Stretching the limbs

Lying on the back naturally, stretch arms and legs

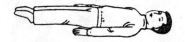

Fig. 1

straight. The ten fingers are also straight. Exert force on the four limbs, and turn the body left and right 5 times (Fig. 1). Or stretch the arms above the head and do the same.

This exercise limbers the joints and muscles of the whole body and invigorates the circulation of the blood.

2. Pulling the knees

(1) Lie on your back with one leg straight and the other bent. Use the hands to pull the bent knee (Fig. 2). Change leg positions and pull other bent knee. Repeat 5 times without interruption.

Fig. 2

This exercise limbers the joints of hips and knees, and also massages the inner organs.

(2) Lie on your back with the right leg straight and the left leg bending. Use both hands to pull the soles of the left foot toward you. Exert force until the knee reaches the chest. A moment later change to the right foot and do the same (Fig. 3).

This exercise limbers the joints of the hip, knees and ankles, and massages the stomach and intestines.

Fig. 3

3. Stretching the feet sideways

Lie on your back. Bend the knees close to each other. Use the hands to pull the feet sideways. Repeat 5 time (Fig. 4).

Fig. 4

This exercise limbers the knees, ankles and lower legs.

4. Arching the back

Lie on your back. Stretch the legs straight. Put your head on a pillow. Using the head and elbows to support the body, bend upward like an arch and turn the body slightly 5 times (Fig. 5).

This exercise limbers the joints of the neck, shoulders, elbows and hip, and strengthens the neck, waist and arm muscles.

The "lying exercises" can be done in bed every morning. They are suitable for old people. They limber up joints and muscles, invigorate the circulation of the blood, massage the inner organs, and promote the normal operation of channels and collaterals. Simple and easy to learn, they are good for postponing aging and for keeping fit.

Fig. 5

Traditional Exercises on the Back: Striking, Rubbing and Kneading

YUAN LIREN

WHEN the weather turns colder, people usually add a vest under a jacket. While sleeping they tuck in the corners of the quit to cover their back. Filial children gently strike the back of elderly people to help them cough up phlegm caught in the trachea. Worried parents often take their babies to doctors to get digestive disorders treated by kneading the muscles along the spine. The back is very important in human health.

Traditional Chinese medicine holds that the back is the protective wall around the inner organs. The *du* vein closely linked with the inner organs and the entire body. The *shu* acupoints along the bladder channel have the function of regulating the *qi* and blood flow, protecting the skin and coordinating the functions of inner organs (heart, liver, spleen, lungs, kidneys, gallbladder, stomach, intestines, bladder and the three visceral cavities). So, proper stimulation on the back can promote the circulation of the *qi* and blood to adapt to changes in the weather, coordinate and strengthen the links between various parts of the body and accelerate the metabolism rate, thus achieving fitness and preventing disease.

Since ancient times medical experts have not only stressed the protection of the back but summed up therapies such as back striking, back rubbing and back kneading as ways of keeping fit and treating ailments. These were recorded in Tang

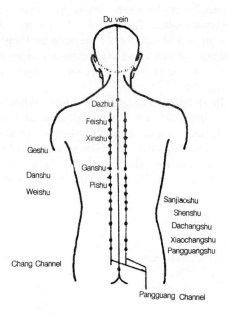

Fig. 1

Dynasty medical classics over a thousand years ago.

1. Back striking

Self striking.

(1) Sit straight. Make fists and strike the back gently along the spine from the waist upward. While striking, slightly bend the body forward. Strike upward as high as possible, then downward to the waist. Repeat the process 5 times without interruption. This exercise can strengthen the heart and adjust the blood pressure, so it is applicable in treating hypertension and heart trouble.

(2) Take a standing position with feet apart. Relax the body. Make hollow fists, the two arms drooping naturally. Swivel the waist, at the same time striking the back and lower abdomen alternately. Repeat 30 times without interruption.

Strike first upward then downward. Exert proper force on fists until you feel comfortable. This exercise can promote the circulation of the *qi* and blood, limber the waist and limbs, improve the functions of the digestive system, and strengthen the kidneys. Weak and old people will become stronger by doing this exercise regularly.

Back striking by others. Sit or lie down. When sitting, bend the body slightly forward. Or lie on the stomach, putting the hands flatly under the forehead. The helper can strike the back from the waist upward, then downward. Exert proper force on the fists so that no pain is felt. This therapy is suitable for the weak and old, and those who find it hard to put their hands back.

2. Back rubbing

Self rubbing. Self rubbing can be done while bathing. Put a wet towel on the back. Grasp the two ends of the towel and rub the back until it feels hot.

Back rubbing by others. Lie on the stomach. Ask the helper to rub along the spine with the palms of the hands until the back feels hot. Too much force should be avoided so as not to graze the skin. Regular practice of this therapy can relieve inner heat and prevent colds. It is effective in bringing down fever, killing pain in waist and back, and alleviating headache caused by colds. Healthy people can do this to prevent a cold, invigorate the functions of the spleen and stomach.

Fig. 2

3. Back kneading

Lie on the stomach. Back naked. Ask someone to knead the skin along the spine by twisting the thumbs and index fingers of the hands alternately from the sacrum upward to the *dazhui* point (see Fig. 2). Repeat three times. This therapy is suitable for both children and adults. It can coordinate the inner organs, invigorate the circulation of the *qi* and blood, improve the functions of the spleen and stomach, and adjust blood pressure. Points to remember: While kneading, don't exert too much force on the fingers, don't move the fingers too fast, and coordinate the fingers harmoniously.

Exercises for Workers Who Stand

YUAN LIREN

S TANDING is a basic posture of the human body. Bench workers, lathe operators, textile workers, compositors, shop clerks, museum guides and school teachers, for example, stand all day long. Standing for long periods of time makes them fatigued and gives them pains in the waist, back and legs, causing varix and swollen legs. An ancient book said that "long time standing injures bones and harms the kidneys." To avoid this, exercises are recommended to invigorate the circulation of the *qi* and blood, and relieve fatigue.

Proceed as follows:

1. Leg swinging. Stand straight. Regulate the breath evenly. Put the hands behind the back. Inhale slowly while

Fig. 1

bending one leg. Then exhale slowly and stretch the leg as if peddling a bicycle. Repeat 10 times without interruption. Change to the other leg and do the same (Fig. 1).

Points to remember: While peddling, the foot should not touch the ground. Inhale while bending the leg and exhale while stretching it. Breathe evenly. This exercise limbers the muscles of the legs and promotes the circulation of blood in them. At the same time it promotes the functions of the stomach and intestines and thus aids digestion.

2. Pulling the foot. Stand straight, legs together. Straighten the knees. Breathe evenly. Put the hands on the back of the waist. Inhale slowly while bending the body backward and exhale slowly while bending the body forward. Then put the arms down. Use the hands to pull the tips of the feet or touch the ground. Keep this posture for a while, then standing straight again. Repeat 10 times (Fig. 2).

Points to remember: Bend the body as far as possible. Inhale while bending backward and exhale while bending forward, coordinating the breath with the actions. This exercise limbers the waist and the joints of the legs, and strengthens the kidneys. Do the exercise slowly.

3. Arm lifting. Stand straight with legs together. Breathe evenly. Clasp the hands before the body. Lift the arms above the head as if lifting a heavy stone, at the same time inhaling

Fig. 2

slowly, followed by constricting the anal muscles. When the arms are raised, turn the palms upward. Exert force on the toes and lift the heels. Keep this posture for a while, then exhale slowly. Turn the waist left and right 5 times. Then go back to the starting position. Repeat the exercise 5 times without interruption (Fig. 3).

Points to remember: Exert enough force on hands and feet. Straighten the legs as much as possible. Inhale while lifting the arms and exhale while turning the waist. When the hands reach the highest point, hold the breath for 2 seconds. When going back to the starting position, relax the body. This exercise limbers the limbs, promotes the circulation of blood in the chest and abdomen, and relieves fatigue.

4. Pressing the legs. Stand straight. Place the left foot on a high place (such as a windowsill). Bend the body forward as far as possible to press the leg. Then use the hands to strike the leg from the ankle, shin and knee to thigh. Strike 10 times. Then change to the right leg and do the same (Fig. 4).

Points to remember: When pressing the leg, both legs

Fig. 3

Fig. 4

should be straight. When striking, exert proper force on the fists. Strike every part of the leg. This exercise limbers the joints and muscles of the legs and is effective for varix and swollen legs caused by long standing.

5. Striking with fist and kicking with foot. Sit straight on a chair. Make fists and place them on the ribs. Inhale slowly. When the lung is full, hold the breath for a while, then exhale fiercely, at the same time striking forward with the left fist and kicking with the right foot. Then change to the right fist and left foot and do the same. Repeat 10 times (Fig. 5).

Points to remember: While striking, put the hollow of the fist downward. While kicking, point the foot upward. Exert force in striking and kicking. Inhale slowly and exhale fiercely. Coordinate the actions with the breath. This exercise limbers the waist and the joints of the shoulders, arms, knees and ankles, and relieve fatigue.

These exercises strengthen the physique, improve the kidney function, invigorate the circulation of the *qi* and blood, and limber muscles and joints. They are effective in relieving fatigue caused by standing for long periods of time. Practicing them regularly in the morning and evening or at work breaks will improve health. It is also suitable for elderly people who have difficulty in walking.

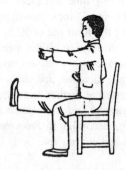

Fig. 5

Walking for Fitness

YUAN LIREN

F OR several thousand years the Chinese people have been walking their way to fitness and health. In traditional Chinese medicine, walking is also seen as a way of preventing as well as treating diseases such as neurasthenia, heart disease, obesity, diabetes and ordinary indigestion. Today the old saying "A walk of 100 paces after meals equals a life of 99 years" is still the rule. In fact, modern Chinese medical experts say that walking is one of the best all-round forms of exercise for health.

The preferred manner of walking is casual and easy-going, with the limbs moving freely in a natural rhythm of joints and muscles. This, combined with a cheerful disposition, is sure to stimulate the circulation of the blood and adjust the functions of the five vital organs of the body.

Walking has drawn adherents from all ages and both sexes because it can be done at any time and place. And for as long as people have been walking, Chinese health experts have offered methods for getting the most out of it.

It is recommended that every walker precede each walk with a relaxing period of warm-up exercises involving the loosening up of the legs, arms, shoulders and back. Deep breathing techniques are also suggested to further relax the body and help clear the mind. Tense muscles and stress detract from the beneficial effects of walking, according to *Proverbs for the Aging*, a book on health published during the Qing Dynasty (1644-1911).

Tang Dynasty (618-907) medical authority Sun Simiao warned that "walking at a quick pace is not suitable." Indeed,

Airing pet birds.

slow even steps create body harmony internally and externally. If the walk seems too dull, one can always choose a more interesting location such as a park with fresh blossoms, a lake mirroring ancient pagodas, or even an exhibition. A friend can also create a more entertaining atmosphere for a walk.

Another ancient medical book from the Sui Dynasty (581-618) recommends that "in the beginning, walk only 120 steps, then increase this to 1,000 steps." Of course, the advantage of walking is that people can adjust the distance and pace to suit their physical condition, and this should be done. It is also very important that the proper clothing is worn: loose and comfortable, and warm enough for the season.

For those who are having trouble falling asleep, a brisk walk of 15 minutes duration after supper is recommended. For people who are angry or overly excited, a slow tranquil walk is in order. A Tang Dynasty book suggests that after meals one should walk to help digest the food (this increases the metabolism rate, which lowers the sugar levels in the bloodstream, thereby helping to prevent and cure diabetes, among other ailments). After the walk, take a nap or sit peacefully.

The most important thing about walking is to do it, and do it regularly. The health benefits do not come immediately but only after walking has become a part of one's daily routine.

Brain Hygiene and Longevity

LIU ZHANWEN

A N OLD maxim says that "life relies on movement." The
movement of the brain is an important factor in health. Li
Shizhen (1518-1593), a great medical expert of the Ming Dynasty, pointed out that "the brain is the headquarters of vital
energy." The health of the brain directly influences all physiological activities of the body. So an ancient expert of life
preservation said that "longevity is closely linked with brain hygiene." Modern research also proves that the brain is the
supreme headquarters of the body; it commands all activities of
systems and organs, and coordinates their functions. It is obvious that a healthy brain is the prerequisite of good health.

How to maintain brain health? Traditional Chinese
medicine holds that an important measure is to use the brain
frequently. Cao Cishan of the Qing Dynasty said, "Never stop
studying because of old age." The brain deteriorates gradually
with the aging process, but frequent use can postpone this,
provide more blood and oxygen to the brain and promote the
growth of brain cells. Scientific research shows that frequent
use of the brain benefits people of all age groups. Mental
workers have a later aging process in the brain cells and a higher intelligence quotient in old age than manual laborers. Sur-
veys outside of China provide convincing data showing that in
old age the intellectuals have a 50 percent higher intelligence
quotient than manual laborers. A vigorous brain can better coordinate the functions of the body, thus strengthening the

Playing chess.

physique and prolonging the life span.

Historically many scholars and experts have had a longer life span than ordinary people. Sun Simiao of the Tang Dynasty wrote a book on medicine at the age of 100. Prof. Ma Yinchu, founder of the new population theory, and a warm advocate of family planning in the 1950s, also lived over a hundred. A survey abroad shows that the average life span of 400 outstanding scientists is 67 years. Those who lived the longest were those who used their brains much, such as Thomas Edison, 84 years; Sir Isaac Newton, 85 years; Albert Einstein, 76 years; Benjamin Franklin, 84 years. Some experts on life prolongation call the hardworking of the brain "keep-fit understanding."

With the rapid development of science and technology, heavy physical labor is becoming less day by day, and mental work is increasing. The influence of this tendency on health has aroused more and more attention and concern. Although many factors influence people's health and longevity, to mental workers scientific use of the brain is more important. Traditional Chinese medicine has accumulated rich experience in this. Here are some items:

1. Brain exercise. Doing brain exercises is very helpful in strengthening the physique and postponing the aging process. The ancients advocated "having wide learning and a retentive memory." Wide learning can increase the memory, while a good memory can widen knowledge, the two promoting each other. To attain this goal, the key lies in the cultivation of interest in study. Experience proves that people can memorize things they are interested in more easily and remember them longer. Scientific experiments show that education at an early age is greatly beneficial to later growth. Elderly people can prevent diseases and postpone the aging process by practicing "brain exercises." At present, various training courses, classes and colleges are open in China for aged people to study. Old people can choose different subjects according to their interests. A rhythmical and regular life is beneficial to health.

2. "Brain bath." We should not only use our brain but adjust it. Every morning after getting up we can have a walk, do morning exercises such as *taijiquan* or *qigong*. Fresh air in the morning provides the brain with more oxygen and awakens nerves and muscles which are in a state of inhibition. When one is tired from study, change the environment, enjoy some music, listen to the songs of birds and the sounds of bubbling streams, or appreciate green grass and beautiful flowers. These activities make one pleasant and invigorate the functions of the brain. This is called "brain bath."

3. Controlling sexual life. Traditional Chinese medicine holds that the kidney channel commands the bones, which produce marrow, which is linked with the brain. The activities of

the brain rely on the nourishment of the kidney channel, which is closely linked with sperm. Zhang Jingyue (1562-1639) of the Ming Dynasty said, "Those who are good at life prolongation will preserve their sperm. By doing so the *qi* flourishes, which makes one vigorous." Controlling sexual life preserves sperm, which is beneficial to the brain, while an excessive sexual life exhausts energy, accelerates the aging process and reduces resistance to disease.

4. Nutrition of the brain. The weight of the brain makes up only 2 percent of the body, but it consumes 20 percent of the body's energy. So it requires a large quantity of nutrition. Brain tissue contains fat, protein, sugar, the vitamin B complex, vitamin C, vitamin E and calcium, of which fat ranks first. Sufficient nutrition for the brain increases the ability of the cerebral cortex to control excitation and inhibition, and thus raises work efficiency. Undernourishment causes a series of ailments.

The following foods contain tonics for the brain: nuts, black sesame seeds, peanuts, beancurd products, corn, millet, dates, pumpkin seeds, chestnuts, honey, quail, marine algae, fish, shrimp and human milk. The nourishment of the brain should start with the embryo. Pregnant women should eat more of these foods, especially vegetarian foods that are beneficial to the growth of the embryo's brain.

A prescription for a tonic for the brain: 1,000 grams of walnut meats, 500 grams of longan and 2,000 grams of honey. Boil the honey, then mix with mashed walnut meats and longan in a jar. Take 30 grams of the mixture twice a day. Continuous use will be effective. Porridges mixed with longan, lotus seeds or dates are also good for the brain.

5. Finger exercises. Finger exercises increase thinking ability and strengthen intelligence. Rotating two metal balls or walnuts in the palm of the hand (called "keep-fit balls") stimulates the brain and the development of its functions, and keeps body balance.

6. Massage. Experts in life prolongation down through the

ages have paid great attention to massage therapy for strengthening the brain. Proceed as follows: Use the fingers as a comb and comb the hair from forehead to the back of the head 12 times. Then use the two thumbs to rub the *taiyang* points clockwise and counterclockwise, each 12 times. Do this morning and evening. Regular practice improves the circulation of the blood in the brain, regulates the channels and veins, increases memory and intelligence, and maintains mental tranquillity.

To keep fit and prolong life, one should live a regular life, give up smoking, keep in a good mood, be optimistic, love life and work hard. This will postpone the aging process and make one vigorous.

Maintaining Normal Excretions of the Body

FU QINGJI

THE body gets rid of harmful waste substances through exhalation, perspiration, urination and defecation. Maintaining normal excretion is an important factor in health and longevity. It is often neglected.

Defecation should take place once every day, though once every other day is also normal. Once every three days is abnormal. Constipation is especially harmful to people with hypertension, coronary heart disease, and hemorrhage of the alimentary canal. Without timely defecation the harmful substances are reabsorbed, a kind of self-poisoning. The longer excrement stays in the colon, the more harmful substances are reabsorbed into the body. This not only harms the organs but irritates the colon and rectum, causing inflammation and sometimes cancer. So we should cultivate the habit of defecating once a day. When constipation occurs, go to doctors and adjust the diet. Eat more vegetables that contain cellulose, such as celery and chives. Add sesame residue and honey. Eat more fruit.

Urinate when urged, never try to hold it. Some harmful substances are discharged through the urine such as creatinine and urea nitrogen. Delayed urination increases the pressure on the bladder, hinders the excretion of urine from the kidney and obstructs the discharge of harmful substances. Long time retention will cause infections of the urinary organs, especially in women, whose urethra is shorter than men. Drinking more water is helpful.

When quiet, a human excretes 800 to 1,500 ml. of water a day through perspiration and exhalation, even though there is no sweat on the skin. Obstacles in these two processes directly harm health. Thus we must protect the skin and maintain its normal functions. We should take a bath often, prevent and treat skin diseases, wear soft garments to keep the body warm in winter, and absorbent clothes with good air permeability in summer. Do exercises regularly to increase vital capacity, keep good ventilation in the room, and have more outdoor activities.

In short, to keep fit, in addition to good nutrition, maintaining normal excretion is very important.

Brain Hygiene for Middle-Aged and Elderly Intellectuals

YANG YINCHANG

B RAIN activity is the basic way mental workers create value in their labor. Thus brain hygiene is especially important for intellectuals.

The ability of the cranial nerves influences various mental activities such as thinking and memory, and is closely linked with mental and physical health. As with other organic parts of the body, the brain begins to decline when a person enters middle age. For most people, the brain cells begin to reduce at the age of 50, and this causes a failing memory and slower reactions. If compounded with diseases such as arterioclerosis, the failing of the brain comes sooner.

If brain debilitation begins before 50, it is called premature senility. Except for physical factors, this is closely connected with psychological factors, particularly the rational use and protection of the brain.

Never Overtaxing the Brain

To protect the brain, one must first of all keep using it.

Excitation and inhibition are the two basic behaviors of the cerebral nerves. The capability of its excitation, the degree of its inhibition and the speed of transition from one to the other are measures of whether the brain is strong or weak. That is to say, a healthy brain should behave according to the objective laws and needs in one state or the other, and transmit promptly.

Although everyone's mental ability has limitations, it is very elastic. As with physical strength, it can be increased through training. The more one uses the brain, the wiser he becomes. But the training should proceed step by step.

Middle-aged people should overcome laziness. This is because physiological changes, such as overweight, have become a burden to various organs and systems of the body. On the other hand, some people may become content with their achievements and reluctant to advance further. Both are harmful to the brain. With the aging process and the decline of physiological functions, laziness will develop, which will accelerate the failing of the brain. Some retirees are not good at arranging their lives, so that within one or two years their aging becomes obvious.

The reduction of brain cells is one reason for the failing of the brain. In a human's lifetime this reduction is insignificant. There are great potentials in the brain that have not been explored. As long as middle-aged and elderly people are willing to use the brain and are good at using it, they can keep a good memory and their efficiency in learning.

The major problem with most middle-aged intellectuals is not laziness but overtaxing the brain. When the brain is tired, one cannot concentrate on anything, thinking is slow, and even dizziness and headaches appear. This is a signal from the transition process in the brain from excitation to inhibition. Fatigue of the brain is a normal phenomenon and can be eliminated with rest. But long-time overtaxing of the brain exceeds the endurance of the brain nerves and may cause brain function disorders, i. e., neurasthenia. So, both laziness and overtaxing of the brain lead to premature senility of the brain. To avoid this, attention must be paid to adjustment of the brain's imbalance.

Adjustment of the Brain

This means proper balance between work and rest as required by the laws of alternative excitation and inhibition of the brain. Generally speaking, a break of 10 minutes once every two hours is necessary. During such breaks, go for a walk or do exercises to inhale fresh air and limber up the joints. These can relieve mental fatigue and tiredness caused by sitting for long periods.

Periodic changes in the form and content of work alternates the excitation and inhibition of different areas of the brain. Such changes result in people not feeling tired even when working for a long time.

Sleep is the protective inhibitor of the brain and is the most important form of rest. Some people think that the older people become, the less they sleep. This is not correct. Middle-aged and elderly intellectuals should guarantee themselves 7 or 8 hours of sleep nightly. Otherwise they cannot recover from the mental work of the day. Long periods of inadequate sleep not only bring on low spirits but also harm the brain.

Adjustment of the brain is not only the need of mental work but an important measure for protecting the brain. Time schedules may vary for different intellectuals but the principle should be "stop for a rest when tired and return to work when recoverd." Pavlov said that "nothing is stronger than rhythm in the activities of the human organism." Regularity in life builds up a rhythm in the excitation and inhibition functions of the brain and makes them adapt to daily life.

Aiding Memory

The first symptom of a failing brain is failing memory, especially recent memory. Almost every old person has this experience: the newly happened things are forgotten easily but the things that happened long ago, even in childhood, can be remembered clearly. Because of this, old people feel it difficult to memorize new things.

Recent memory is short-term memory, the initial stage of memory. After learning new things, the middle-aged and elderly should consolidate them, turning short-term memory into long-term memory. They should take advantage of their accumulated knowledge, connect the newly learned knowledge with old knowledge to help memorize it. Another method is to take notes, which are not only convenient to check but helpful to memory. In fact, everyone can devise methods of his own to raise memory ability. A good memory is not only the need of mental work, it is one of the measures of saving effort and keeping the brain fit.

Keeping in a Good Mood

The psychological changes in the middle-aged and elderly intellectuals are great. Middle-aged people are often nervous because of the double burden of career and family. When entering old age, the division of their family, the separation from their offspring and the reduction of social activities make them lonely. Weaker physique, illness and fewer interests in life may cause depression and vexation, which are harmful to health and the functions of the brain.

People who live long often have different secrets, but a common one is keeping in a good mood and being optimistic. Continuing to learn helps relieve depression but cannot eliminate it. When worried, it is important to comfort oneself and not allow the worries to linger in the mind. Second, keep some hobbies, such as chess, painting and calligraphy, raising flowers, fishing and so on. These help adjust the brain and improve one's mental state. Third, pursue a perfect life. This includes not only one's career but marriage and family. Even in old age, single people should find a marriage partner, the widowed should organize a new family. Fourth, pay attention to appearance. "Slovenly" is often used to describe some intellectuals. Taking care of appearance and clothing awakens vigor. Fifth, enjoy family happiness. Middle-aged and elderly intellectuals should not become unsociable and eccentric. Besides social activities, they should entertain together with children and young people, a process that makes them forget their years.

Strengthening Physique

Except for physiological and psychological factors, physical condition is another important factor influencing the health of the brain. Adequate nutrition, a rational diet, giving up smoking and alcohol are all necessary. Emphasis should also be placed on the most effective method of strengthening the physique — sports.

Sports is commonly recognized as the most effective method of preventing and treating disease and prolonging life. Statistics show that with people between 40 and 50 there are great differences in physical condition between those who persist in sports and those who don't. Continued participation in sports or manual labor can prolong a life by 10 years on the average. Sports strengthen the physique and temper the will, improve the state of mind and coordinate the functions of the organs and systems of the body. It reduces obesity and blood fat, and prevents and treats arteriosclerosis. For mental workers, movement can relieve mental fatigue, accelerate the metabolism rate, raise the capability of the brain to control the excitation and inhibition function, and bring good sleep.

Finally, although most people admit that exercise, entertainment, diet and sleep are important to mental health, many do not pay enough attention to them because of tight time schedules. Yet spending time on exercises raises work efficiency and wins more time for work. This is the dialectical logic of time consumption.

Massage Therapy for Insomnia

WEN JIAO

HERE are two massage therapies for insomnia caused by neurasthenia.

1. Take a sitting position. Press the finger on the *sanyinjiao* acupuncture point 3.9 inches above the inner ankle bone just behind the edge of the tibia (Fig. 1) 30 times. A feeling of soreness or swelling shows the massage is being done at the correct point.

Lie on your back. Press with the hand alternately the *shenmen* points (on the small finger side, in the depression just at the end of the transverse crease of the wrist (Fig. 2) until a feeling of soreness or swelling occurs.

Lie on your stomach. Make fists. Overlap them and place them on the area between the *shangwan* and *zhongwan* acu-

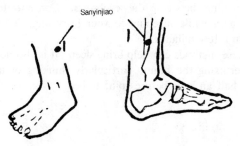

Sanyinjiao

Fig. 1

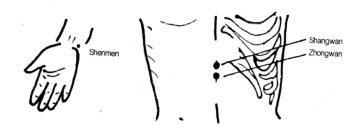

Fig. 2   Fig. 3

points (the *shangwan* is 6.5 inches and the *zhongwan* 5.2 inches above the navel, see Fig. 3). Let the body weigh naturally on the overlapped fists for three minutes while concentrating on the pressed area.

Lie on the left side and breathe deeply several times. Be sure you are breathing evenly, slowly, deeply and naturally. Don't hold the breath.

Lie on the right side. Breathe deeply several times in the same manner before returning to the natural body position. Soon you will sleep.

2. Alternately press the *shenmen* points on both wrists 30 times. Lie in a comfortable position. Make a loose fist (left or right) and place it on the forehead with the protruding hard part touching between the eyebrows. Concentrate on the pressed area while listening to your breathing. You will fall asleep in a few minutes.

These methods can help bring sleep. It is also necessary to stop overtaxing the brain, particularly thinking of unpleasant things, half an hour before going to bed.

Massage Therapy for Hypertension

WEN JIAO

HIGH blood pressure is one of the common symptoms of arteriosclerosis and heart disease. Because it arises from many factors, it should be treated in many ways. In addition to acupuncture, medicines and diet, massage at acupuncture points is also effective.

A theory of traditional Chinese medicine holds that with symptoms occurring in the upper part of the body, treatment should be given to the lower part. Since the symptoms of hypertension are often headache and dizziness, the first self-massage therapy is to rub *yongquan* point on the underside of the foot (Fig. 1), which has the function of lowering blood pres-

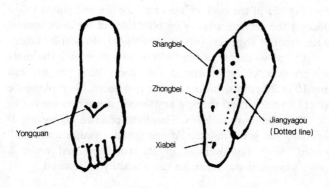

Fig. 1   **Fig. 2**

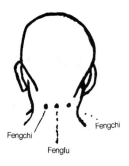

Fengchi

Fengchi

Fengfu

Fig. 3

sure.

Here are two massage therapies:

1. Massage the underside of the arches of the foot every day before getting up in the morning and going to bed at night. Take a sitting position. With the thumb (or the heel of the other foot) vigorously rub the *yongquan* acupoint in the direction of the toes 100 times (about two minutes).

2. Massage the head and neck. Place palms on forehead, press and squeeze toward the back of the head. Turn hands over, palms up, and massage with the outer side of the small fingers from above the ears downward through the *jiangyagou line* (Fig. 2) at the back of the ears, the *fengchi* points (Fig. 3) along the cervical arteries on both sides of the neck around to the front of the chest (about 30 seconds). Repeat 20 times.

These two therapies can be done in any order. The massage brings a feeling of ease in the head. Blood pressure can drop 10 or 20 points, lasting four or five hours. To prolong the effect, do the second therapy any time it seems necessary.

These are easy to learn. Persistent practice, however, is necessary for good results. At the outset, medication is still needed. With improvement of the condition and under a doctor's instructions, medicine can gradually be reduced.

An Exercise for Piles

WEN JIAO

H EMORRHOIDS, one of man's most common problems, can be alleviated with a therapeutic exercise advocated centuries ago in China. It involves regularly constricting the anal muscles to give a better blood circulation and tone to the tissues. As a matter of fact, the exercise is an essential movement in *qigong* (breathing) and *taijiquan* (boxing) movements.

The method consists of four points: (1) breathing in, (2) putting the tip of the tongue on the palate, (3) constricting the anal muscles, and (4) holding the breath.

One proceeds as follows: Relax the body. Press the thighs together and make an effort to close the buttocks. Breathe in while raising the tip of the tongue to the palate, at the same time constricting the anal muscles. Hold the breath for a moment. Then breathe out and relax before repeating the movements.

The exercise can be done anywhere and in any body position — sitting, lying or standing. It is best done at fixed hours every day, at least once in the morning and once in the evening, each time repeating the movements until one begins to tire.

Points to remember:

1. Those with anal fissures, inflammation or abscess around the anus should not do the exercise until these are healed.

2. Do the exercise daily without interruption.

3. Avoid eating hot and spicy foods.

4. Don't delay bowel movements.

5. Avoid strain and constipation.

6. Better results are often obtained by combining this exercise with *qigong* routines or supplementing them with warm baths, hot compresses or massage.

Massage Eases Meniere's Disease

WEN JIAO

T HE CAUSE of attacks of Meniere's syndrome is not yet understood. The symptoms are dizziness, ringing in the ears and deafness associated with the labyrinth of the ear. In most cases it occurs when physically or mentally overtired. Here is a simple but effective massage therapy for it.

1. Massage in order each of the following acupuncture points 20 times — *yintang*, *meiyao*, *sizhukong*, *tongziliao*, *taiyang*, *shangguan*, *ermen*, *qubin* and *chengqi* (Fig. 1).

2. Massage for period of normalcy (intervals between attacks): Press these same points in order but do the key points — *tongziliao*, *taiyang*, *shangguan* and *ermen* — 30 times each, half again as many as the other points.

Proceed as follows:

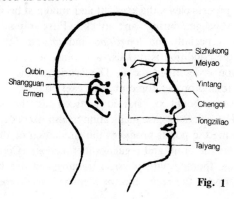

Fig. 1

Fig. 2

Close eyes. Make loose fists with thumbs on middle fingers. Stretch out index fingers for pressing the points. Rotate them in a circle clockwise (Fig. 2). Concentrate your mind, press slowly with proper force (too lightly produces little effect, too much brings a feeling of discomfort). Except the *yintang* between the eyebrows the corresponding points on both sides should be pressed at the same time.

Next run your index or middle fingers from the *tongziliao* point backwards through the *taiyang*, *shangguan* to the *ermen*. Repeat as many times as necessary.

The process clears the eyesight and mind and brings relief.

3. Massage during an attack: First press the key acupoints, especially the *tongziliao* and *taiyang* for a longer time. If the condition is serious, ask someone to do the massage for you as described above. The location of the points must be accurate and proper force must be exerted.

Massage should be started as soon as the symptoms appear. For a serious case medication is also needed.

Pressing the points promotes the circulation of the *qi* and blood, rests the brain and regulates its functions. Coordinating the massage therapy with physical training and rest helps still more to prevent the recurrence of Meniere's syndrome.

126

'Swinging in the Sea'

WEN JIAO

THIS exercise, the *huanghai* (swinging in the sea), is popular in China because it is very effective in treating many diseases, especially insomnia, dream-disturbed sleep, and intestinal and gastric disorders such as constipation and loose bowels.

It requires sitting still and then gently swiveling the upper part of the body to benefit the internal organs, limbs and bones. It helps to strengthen the functions of the viscera, regulate the blood flow, and promote the normal operation of the channels and their collaterals through which the *qi* circulates.

The *huanghai* exercise is simple and easy to learn. Anyone, whether old, weak or ill, can do it provided he can take a sitting position.

Proceed as follows:

An ordinary sitting position or sit cross-legged. Place the hands above the knees. Sit still, straight but relaxed, head upright, facing directly forward. Remain in this position for a few minutes. Bend toward the right, then swivel to the left, straighten up and return to starting position. Repeat 36 times without interruption. Then bend toward the left and swivel to the right, straighten up and return to starting position. Continue 36 times.

Points to remember:

1. If taking an ordinary sitting position, it is better to use a stool. Sit on the edge with legs apart to shoulder width, feet parallel and pointing straight forward.

2. If sitting cross-legged, turn from right to left when the left leg is on top; turn from left to right when the right leg is on top; changing leg position for reverse directions.

3. Bend and swivel with the waist as the axis, nose pointing toward the navel. Don't raise your head.

4. The degree of the bend depends on the condition or degree you think fit. Those suffering dizziness, hypertension or a feeling of repression in the chest need not bend far, those with body aches may bend lower, and those with intestinal or gastric trouble may bend moderately.

5. Do the exercise slowly, evenly, and in a relaxed way, concentrating your mind as if you were a part of the vast sea of air and swinging in it — hence the name "Swinging in the Sea."

The *huanghai* exercise is used in treating ailments and also for maintaining good health. In the former case, many such sessions are required daily and the number of times for swiveling should be increased slowly. In the latter case, it is enough to do the exercise only once before going to bed at night, repeating the process 36 times for each side, lasting about 15 minutes.

Therapy for Shoulder and Back Ache

WEN JIAO

PAIN from functional disorders in the shoulder and lumbar regions is mainly caused by muscle spasms, inflammation or tissue contraction. Traditional Chinese medicine holds that such pain occurs when there is obstruction of the blood and *qi* caused by an attack of cold or wind on the corresponding area of the body. Hence, heat is required to promote blood circulation. The striking therapy below is based in this theory and is effective in alleviating shoulder and lumbar pain.

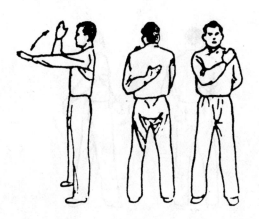

Fig. 1   Fig. 2

1. Striking the arms alternately: Spread the legs naturally. Raise one arm horizontally in front of the body (it is not necessary to keep it straight). Strike it with the palm of the other hand from the shoulder all the way down to the hand, then repeat in the reverse direction. The strikings should be done first with the arm held palm downward, then again with the right edge of the hand upward, and a third time with the palm upward (Fig. 1).

2. Striking the shoulders and back: Spread the legs naturally. While striking the left shoulder with the right palm, strike the right part of the back with the back of the left hand. While striking the right shoulder with the palm of the left hand, strike the left part of the back with the back of the right hand (Fig. 2).

3. Striking the *shenshu* points: Spread the legs naturally. Strike these acupoints alternately with the palm or back of the hand or with the fist — two inches lateral to the lower border of the spinous process of the second lumbar vertebra (Fig. 3).

4. Swinging and striking the waist: Spread the legs natu-

Fig. 3   Fig. 4

rally in a relaxed posture. While swinging the arms and waist to one side and then the other, strike the lumbar region with one hand and then the other with the back of the hand (Fig. 4).

Points to remember:

1. Striking must gradually become heavier. Do the exercises slowly. Avoid strain.

2. The length of time and the number of times vary with the constitution of the exerciser. Repeat the movements until the stricken area feels warm and comfortable, generally two to four sessions daily, each lasting about 20 minutes.

3. The amount of exercise must be moderate. When the relevant muscle begins to ache and a feeling of heaviness occurs when raising the arms, the amount can be increased, because this is considered a normal physiological reaction. When local symptoms of pain begin to appear and become more and more serious — an indication that there must be latent inflammation in the muscle or tendon — the amount should be reduced. Stop immediately when there is a feeling of numbness somewhere, a sign that the way you are doing the exercise is wrong and has caused nervous constriction. Discontinue until you discover the reason and can do them correctly.

Hand Workouts with Metal Balls

WEN JIAO

I T IS common in China to see elderly people strolling or chatting while turning two polished metal balls in one hand. The clicking of the balls gives a clear, musical sound. These are what the old folks call "keep-fit balls." The Chinese Premier presented U. S. President Reagan and Mrs. Reagan each with a pair as a gift during their visit to China in 1984.

Keep-fit balls can be traced back to the Ming Dynasty about 500 years ago. They first appeared as solid balls used for exercise and to defend oneself. They gradually developed into hollow balls with something like a clapper inside to produce a sound when turned, and were mainly used for keeping fit. Some elderly people use walnuts or wooden balls instead.

The keep-fit ball exercise is simple and easy to do. Place the balls in the palm of the right hand and rotate them counterclockwise with the five fingers. Then change to the other hand and rotate them clockwise. Practice until they can be manipulated smoothly. A skillful exerciser can operate three or four balls in one hand at the same time and perform in several different ways.

The exercise helps to stimulate flood circulation and relaxes the muscles and joints. If done regularly, some say, it also regulates central cerebral nerves and improves memory. It is helpful in preventing and treating numbness in the hands, trembling, finger or wrist arthritis and hypertension.

According to traditional Chinese medicine's theories on

the channels and their collaterals through which the *qi* flows, on the five fingers of each hand there are a number of acu-points connected to several channels. These channels link the cerebral nerves with viscera. Symptoms manifested in a certain internal organ immediately reflect along a certain channel.

The keep-fit ball exercise, through regular movements of the hands, is aimed at promoting the normal operation of the channels, regulating the *qi* and blood circulation, and benefit-ing internal organs. The friction between the balls in motion and between the balls and the palm produces static electricity and heat which stimulate the channels, and therefore it is be-lieved useful in treating ailments in many parts of the body.

Waist Swivel

WEN JIAO

T HE waist-swivel exercise (*zhuan yao gong*) is simple and easy, and helpful in cases of chronic constipation and poor intestinal function.

There are many causes for habitual constipation — working for long hours seated, lack of physical exercise or manual labor, living an irregular life, lack of fiber in the diet, and not drinking enough water. The foremost one, however, is the lack of physical exercise over a long period. This weakens the elasticity of the muscles of the diaphragm, abdomen and anus which, when functioning normally, coordinate to move the bowels, and leads to insufficient intestinal peristalsis.

This exercise, through toning some of the muscles in the lumbar, abdominal and pelvic regions, is aimed at strengthening the muscles of the abdominal wall and increasing the secretion of intestinal juices to promote peristalsis.

Proceed as follows:

Starting position: Spread legs to a width a little greater than the shoulders, feet pointing slightly outward and hands on hips. Keep the upper part of the body straight with knees slightly bent (Fig. 1).

Movements: With the navel as the axis, swivel mainly the lumbar and abdominal regions in the following directions:

1. First swivel horizontally in a clockwise direction: left, front, right, back (see line with arrow, Fig. 2).

2. Then do the same counterclockwise (see dotted line with arrow, Fig. 2).

3. Now pretend your midsection is a wheel and turn it vertically from the left: left, down, right, up (see dotted line

with arrow, Fig. 3).

4. Then do the same in the other direction (see the line with arrow, Fig. 3).

Points to remember:

1. Swivel mainly the lumbar and abdominal regions, not the shoulders and knees.

2. Start by doing the exercise once a day. This may gradually be increased to three times daily according to the constitution and condition of the exerciser.

Fig. 1   Fig. 2

Fig. 3

'Stepping Back' for Lumbar Pain

WEN JIAO

P AIN from muscle and ligament strain in the lumbar region is frequently a problem for people past middle age. Therapeutic exercises can help this kind of backache. "Stepping back" is one of these.

"Stepping back" is based on a movement in China's traditional *taijiquan* boxing. It consists mainly of backing up a number of steps at a time while pressing the *shenshu* points on the back (see diagram). This also benefits the kidneys. Backward movements keeping the torso straight are also effective in preventing and treating stooped posture.

Proceed as follows:

Starting position: Stand straight, chest out and head up, facing forward. Place hands on hips with the thumbs on the back pressing the *shenshu* points, fingers in front.

Movements: Start with the left leg. Lift it as high as possible without losing your balance and step back, shifting the body's center of gravity in the same direction. Let the ball of the left foot touch the ground first, then the whole foot. Shift your weight to the left leg and step back with the right leg in the same way. Repeat these movements, starting by doing them three times, and over a period of time build up to a greater number.

Nose Massage

WEN JIAO

H ERE is a useful therapy for sinusitis and rhinitis.
Starting position: Sit straight facing directly forward. Concentrate your attention (Fig. 1).

Exercise 1: Pressing the *baihui* point.

Bring the right index, middle and ring fingers together and press light on the *baihui* point (Fig. 2). Rotate fingers clockwise. Repeat 60 times until there is a feeling of coolness in the nose.

Exercise 2: Massaging the bridge of the nose.

Using the index and middle fingers of both hands, massage the sides of the bridge near the inner corners of the eyes. Squeeze and press gently in an up-and-down direction (Fig. 3). Repeat 60 times for rhinitis and 80 times for sinusitis. A feeling of relief and comfort should follow.

Exercise 3: Pressing the *yingxiang* points (Fig. 4) on either side of the nostrils. Rotate tips of fingers. Repeat 60 times for rhinitis and 70 times for sinusitis. This should clear blocked passages and make breathing easier.

Exercise 4: Massaging the *yintang*, *yangbai*, *sizhukong* and *taiyang* points.

Run the index, middle and ring fingers of both hands simultaneously from the *yintang* point in the center of the forehead outward through the *yangbai* and *sizhukong* to the *taiyang* points (Fig. 5). Repeat 60 times. Slight swelling and numbness should accompany relief.

After finishing these four exercises, repeat the whole set twice. Three sessions daily, morning, afternoon and evening are recommended, the whole set done three times per session. Following this regimen for two weeks should produce beneficial results.

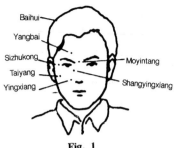

Fig. 1

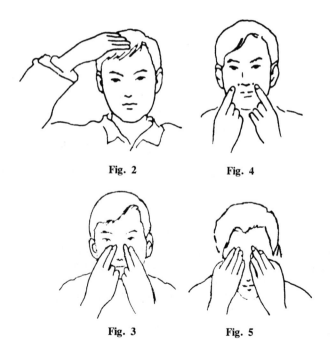

Fig. 2   **Fig. 4**

Fig. 3   **Fig. 5**

Treating a Stiff Neck

WEN JIAO

A STIFF neck caused by injured soft tissues of the cervical region is a common problem, especially for middle-aged men. It occurs more frequently in the spring and winter, with pain in one or both sides of the neck. Turning the head sharpens the pain, which may spread to one side of the shoulder or back. Examinations reveal obvious tender points in the affected areas and muscle spasms. But there is no deformity of the cervical vertebrae.

Traditional Chinese medicine believes that this is caused by cold, an awkward sleeping position or sleeping after becoming overtired. In the latter case, the pain in the cervical muscles, which have been stretched in the same position for long hours, produces strain and spasms.

Below is a simple therapy for this ailment. Combining hot compresses with massage of the head and neck, and slow cervical movements should eliminate the symptoms within a few

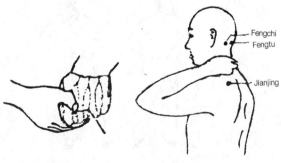

Fengchi
Fengtu

Jianjing

Fig. 1   Fig. 2

days.

Self-massage therapy:

Alternately press with the thumbs the *laozhen* points on both hands between the second and third metacarpal bones (Fig. 1) for one minute until a swollen feeling appears. Rub your hands together to warm them. Then use them alternately to rub the back of the neck 20 times each. Massage the *fengchi* and *jianjing* points (Fig. 2) 20 times each, as well as the muscles along the cervical vertebrae as much as seems necessary.

Cervical vertebrac exercises:

1. Slowly raise the head, lower it, and then turn it from left to right (don't force this movement if it brings too much pain). Repeat 25 times. Then do the same in the other direction.

2. Spread the legs to shoulder width (or take a sitting position) with both hands on the hips. Turn the head to the left and then upwards as much as you can, with eyes turning in the same direction. Return to the starting position and repeat motions on the right side. Inhale while turning and exhale while returning to the starting position (Fig. 3).

Following the whole procedure once generally alleviates pain and the condition is improved by the next day. If this is not the case, repeat the therapy the following morning and evening.

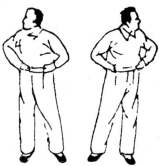

Fig. 3

责任编辑：艾　杉
图片编辑：张敬德
装帧设计：武　悦
校　订：刘宗仁　何俊龙

Editor: Ai Shan
Layont Design: Wu Yue
Revisors: Liu Zongren
　　　　　He Junlong

实用中医养生(英)

＊

今日中国出版社出版
(中国北京百万庄路 24 号)
外文印刷厂印刷
中国国际图书贸易总公司发行
(中国北京车公庄西路 35 号)
北京邮政信箱第 399 号　邮政编码 100044
1989 年第 1 版第 1 次印刷
1997 年第 2 版第 1 次印刷
ISBN　7－5072－0902－4/R·20
14－E－2326P
02400